—— T H E ——
McGRAW-HILL
36-Hour Course

PRODUCT
DEVELOPMENT

Other books in The McGraw-Hill 36-Hour Course series:

PRODUCT DEVELOPMENT

Andrea Belz, Ph.D., M.B.A.

New York   Chicago   San Francisco   Lisbon   London   Madrid   Mexico City
Milan   New Delhi   San Juan   Seoul   Singapore   Sydney   Toronto

The McGraw·Hill Companies

Copyright © 2011 by The McGraw-Hill Companies, Inc. All rights reserved. Printed in the United States of America. Except as permitted under the United States Copyright Act of 1976, no part of this publication may be reproduced or distributed in any form or by any means, or stored in a database or retrieval system, without the prior written permission of the publisher.

1 2 3 4 5 6 7 8 9 10 11 12 13 14 15   QFR/QFR   1 9 8 7 6 5 4 3 2 1 0

ISBN   978-0-07-174387-7
MHID   0-07-174387-1

This publication is designed to provide accurate and authoritative information in regard to the subject matter covered. It is sold with the understanding that neither the author nor the publisher is engaged in rendering legal, accounting, securities trading, or other professional services. If legal advice or other expert assistance is required, the services of a competent professional person should be sought.

> —*From a Declaration of Principles Jointly Adopted by a Committee of the American Bar Association and a Committee of Publishers and Associations*

Library of Congress Cataloging-in-Publication Data

Belz, Andrea.
   The McGraw-Hill 36-hour course : product development / by Andrea Belz.
       p.   cm.
   Includes index.
   ISBN: 978-0-07-174387-7 (alk. paper)
   1. New products.   2. Product management.   I. Title.

   HF5415.153.B45   2011
   658.5'75—dc22   2010042594

Trademarks: McGraw-Hill, the McGraw-Hill Publishing logo, 36-Hour Course, and related trade dress are trademarks or registered trademarks of The McGraw-Hill Companies and/or its affiliates in the United States and other countries and may not be used without written permission. All other trademarks are the property of their respective owners. The McGraw-Hill Companies is not associated with any product or vendor mentioned in this book.

McGraw-Hill books are available at special quantity discounts to use as premiums and sales promotions or for use in corporate training programs. To contact a representative, please e-mail us at bulksales@mcgraw-hill.com.

This book is printed on acid-free paper.

CONTENTS

ACKNOWLEDGMENTS

Product development is many things, but it's really about coordinating people of diverse talents. Although I hope this book will be enlightening, this topic is best taught by example; thus, your early interactions can inform much of your career.

I have always been fortunate to learn from extremely talented colleagues. While I learned from each and every client and enjoyed working with them all, Jim Cutts, Malcolm Cloyd, and Chuck Moffitt were particularly generous in giving their time to mentor me. My friends at the Pasadena Angels welcomed me early in my career and shared their insights; I have enjoyed a particularly interesting experience as the organization's longest-serving woman (I just can't write "the oldest woman"). My protracted education put me in front of many talented instructors, but a few stood head and shoulders above the rest (certainly above me), sharing their insights with both humor and rigor: Phil Roos and Bob McKeown taught me the importance of thinking, speaking, and writing with clarity, while Dave McMahon and Jack Green demonstrated a disciplined approach to business management. I followed Dave and Jack's example through my extensive use of case studies drawn from the Harvard Business School, Stanford Graduate School of Business, and the University of Hong Kong. Although they are not to be taken as primary sources, these documents illustrate the rich diversity of practice at some of the world's leading corporations.

Many people generously shared their expertise, including Eric P. Rose, NPDP, consultant and adjunct professor of product innovation at Pepperdine University; Ross Epstein, head of the Intellectual Property Enforcement Practice at The Nath Law Group; and Jeffrey Sheldon, managing director of the intellectual property law firm Sheldon, Mak, and Anderson. Bill Matthies, entrepreneur and marketing guru, helped me articulate some of my ideas, and Rich Allen was always available to listen to my rants. I owe very special thanks to operations guru and insightful friend Lisa Anderson, who suspected I had more to say than I previously thought, and to Michele Wells, the acquisitions editor who agreed with Lisa. Brian Foster and Nancy Hall at McGraw-Hill guided me in bringing this manuscript to completion and encouraged me to continue writing. My graphic artist, Farrukh Ali of creativebugss, has demonstrated that as the world gets smaller, your ability to build and sustain relationships matters as much as, if not more than, your product.

And now, dessert. My inspiration comes from my sons, Nicholas and Stephen, who tolerated my high level of distraction by simply being more distracting, and for that, I thank them. They remind me daily that it is easier to build a cathedral when one starts with the finest marble. Finally, I wish to express humble thanks to Eric, my husband and partner. None of this would be possible without him.

INTRODUCTION

Have you ever driven off to work, realized you have forgotten your cell phone, and returned home to fetch it? It is amazing to remember that until fifteen years ago, a phone that you carried wherever you went was a fantasy; for a couple of years, it was a luxury. Now it has taken its rightful place with your wallet and keys as an item you absolutely have with you at all times.

Truly revolutionary items are uncommon, but we are overwhelmed with products and associated advertising. A typical supermarket has 45,000 different products,[1] so if you go grocery shopping on a regular basis, you experience that bewildering diversity every week. The A.C. Nielsen Company reports that the average child sees 20,000 30-second television commercials per year.[2] How can your product cut through the mess and stand out?

Traditional product development is taught as a "sink-or-swim" methodology. The few business schools that offer product development classes use them as a laboratory for teams to develop products and associated business plans, then pitch them to investors. In the real world, however, systematic product development exists. Several organizations have refined the process with clear steps that can be taught easily; you can reduce your risk of sinking if you learn about these excellent companies.

This book is based on the concept that product development is where innovation meets customer needs. Part 1 begins with a deep strategic analysis to help you understand the marketplace and determine how to use corporate strengths to exploit opportunities. Subsequent chapters detail methodologies for identifying and protecting these opportunities, as well as approaches for funding a product development project.

Part 2 addresses implementation and organizational challenges. There is an introduction to the product track, derived from Michael Porter's value chain and emphasizing the role of design, and then a description of the various elements of fabrication, integration, and delivery for both capital goods and software companies. Later chapters address effective communication programs, and the book closes with some personal observations made over many years of helping organizations with all phases of development projects.

Throughout the book, the text emphasizes the role of risk reduction because this is probably management's top priority. Product development is inherently fraught with uncertainty; inexperienced managers often "don't know what they don't know" and are poorly prepared to face these challenges. In the spirit of teaching by example, I draw extensively on case studies, integrating them with explanations of traditional marketing theory, organizational behavior, and technology management practice to create a comprehensive picture of product development. Many of these processes can be implemented anywhere; every company has the opportunity to become a creative, efficient force if it is managed properly.

This book is written for anyone with inventive ideas who is interested in walking through the entire product development cycle, from experienced managers to young innovators. Since creative people with neat product concepts sometimes have an entrepreneurial streak, I have included additional information for this group. I also address topics related to service providers, because product development issues—from the need to offer a compelling value proposition to the realities of outsourcing—are universal.

My goal is to show you that innovation is not accidental, and that with the right tools, everyone can manage an effective process combining creativity and discipline for great results. I hope you enjoy the journey as much as I have.

THE
McGRAW-HILL
36-Hour Course

PRODUCT
DEVELOPMENT

1

PLANNING: DRESS FOR SUCCESS

Taken from start to finish, the product development process presents a challenge to everyone, from a creative visionary to a detail-oriented perfectionist. People often talk in grand terms about the 30,000-foot view, forgetting that the plane starts at ground level. Reality calls for working on the details from the beginning. Every general thinks carefully about ensuring supply chains and logistics for his troops before the battle begins, even while he is surveying the terrain to understand the battlefield and searching for advantages.

Part 1 of this book is concerned with the existential side of product development: why does this product need to exist? Chapter 1 describes inception by broadly defining a product in terms of the dynamics of supply and demand, as well as identifying the sources of associated risk. Chapter 2 explores the formal strategy of selecting the path where corporate strengths can most effectively exploit marketplace opportunities; this chapter describes tools to help you identify both internal and external environments where there is room for growth.

Chapters 3 and 4 provide an overview of marketing. Chapter 3 develops the fundamentals of marketing theory, including segmentation, targeting, and positioning; it then covers the classic marketing Four Ps. Chapter 4 introduces the concept of a value proposition and relates it to corporate strategy, then walks through several pricing schemes to demonstrate how attractive products become compelling revenue models.

Chapter 5 addresses the key component of creating sustainable competitive advantage through protected intellectual property. It covers the various types of protection and then describes various monetization schemes.

Finally, the strategic portion of the book closes with Chapter 6, which explains the basic principles of capital budgeting to help you determine how to maximize your chances for funding success. It is based on the understanding that competition consists of all deals on the table at one time.

Part 1 creates the building blocks for Part 2 and sets the stage for efficient planning for growth. The entrepreneur-visionary and the marketing expert with a strong economic bent will both benefit from this review of the context for successful product development.

1

INCEPTION

A journey of a thousand miles must begin with a single step.

—LAO TZU

very day you are assaulted with new products. You might start your day with a new variety of corn flakes. Perhaps you are considering buying an electronic book reader. Or your lawyer calls to tell you that he now does estate plans in addition to wills. New products come at you all day, every day.

How can you join the fray with your new product? More important, how can you rise above the fray?

This book describes the entire product development process from first idea to successful launch. It explains basic concepts from strategy and engineering to design and finance using real-life examples to illustrate both successes and failures.

People enter this path for many reasons. Maybe you are a born entrepreneur who is captivated by the vision of creating something out of nothing. Perhaps you are a product manager in a large organization and have just learned that margins on your existing products have shrunk, leading to the terrifying conclusion that you need something new. Or you could be an inventor toiling away in a laboratory who has just stumbled on a development that could actually change people's lives.

You may be a lawyer, an accountant, or a consultant whose clients have asked you to provide a novel service—and you may be able to standardize your new product, reproducing it quickly and profitably. This is why people talk about turning products into "cookie-cutter models"—products that are identical and quickly replicated.

Historically, product development has been taught on an ad hoc basis, with most classroom work involving team projects. That is obviously not the approach taken in this book, although it can be used in conjunction with team activities. Instead, it focuses on helping you develop insights on your own, taking hints from examples in the current business press.

DEFINITION OF A PRODUCT

There are many ways to consider a product. A simple definition is that a product is an independently priced item that provides value to a customer. Sometimes it is a service, such as a private school that offers new after-school care in addition to regular classes. In other cases, it may be different packaging of an existing product, such as the Hershey's Kiss, which is made from the same chocolate as the company's classic candy bar but in a smaller size and different shape.

CONCEPT

What Is a Product?
A *product* is an independently priced item that provides value to a customer.

HINT

Products for Service Providers
Service providers still offer products if they offer independently priced items for a set fixed fee. Examples include an accountant's fixed price for an audit or a lawyer's standard fee for creating a will. This explains why hourly consulting can be problematic; if your product is an hour of time, you need to demonstrate that your hourly output has value greater than the hourly rate.

In its most basic form, a product must link a capability and a solution, as shown in Figure 1-1. There are many other ways to think of a product. For instance, from a strong marketing viewpoint, a product provides another link between the provider and the customer. This works for companies with strong brands seeking to offer a suite of solutions to the same customers. Some companies don't have powerful consumer brands but still maintain good reputations in a narrow technical niche, such as electronics manufacturing or a legal specialty; they may seek to cultivate their relationships with their customers by offering another product.

Who Makes Products?

Broadly speaking, three categories of professionals make products:

- **Product managers:** Managers in large organizations who are responsible for a single product line or group of products. These people are typically part of a complex hierarchy and respond to larger organizational dynamics.
- **Entrepreneurs:** Individuals seeking to launch new companies based on an initial product. These people often moonlight, using their spare time to refine their product ideas and evaluate the feasibility of different business models.
- **Service providers:** Accountants, lawyers, consultants, bankers, and other professionals who provide services rather than manufactured goods. These people can develop new products rather rapidly because they do not have the limitations of capital equipment or inventory, but they must still be aware of all the other management elements required for success.

Figure 1-1   A Product Links a Capability and a Solution

Throughout this book, all of these groups will be described as "innovators." However, when issues with different implications for each type of business arise, they will be addressed independently.

Some Innovations Are Not Products

Every year, *BusinessWeek* and Boston Consulting Group jointly produce a list of the 50 most innovative companies in the world. They then classify the companies with respect to the innovation: process, product, business model, or customer experience. In 2009, only 15 of the top 50 appeared on the list because of product innovations; the rest innovated in other aspects of their business.[1]

Consider some of the entries. As you might expect, the top company, Apple, appeared on the list for its product. General Electric, which was number 6 in 2006[2] for product and process, dropped to number 17 in 2009 for process alone. Google came out at number 2 in 2006 for its business model and in 2009 for its customer experience. Meanwhile, Wal-Mart appeared on the list at number 20 in 2006 for its innovative processes, but by 2009, it had vanished.

Following the gyrations of these companies shows us two interesting dynamics:

1. Innovation is not limited to product design.
2. Even creative companies can become complacent and lose their edge.

MINICASE

To Italy for a Cappuccino!
When Starbucks founder Howard Schultz went to Italy in the early 1980s, he was captivated by the Italian café experience and wanted to bring it to the United States. At that time, his partners, who were focused on coffee roasting, were not so enthralled. Ultimately the management team split, and Schultz continued to refine his model. His revelation transformed how we experience the neighborhood coffeehouse; at the same time, he transformed the economics of coffee drinking, as customers began paying $4.00 for something that had previously cost $0.50. Even though Schultz's actual product was marvelous Italian coffee drinks, it also included the delightful—and highly

predictable—environment of each store. (Chapter 3 discusses marketing and the added value you can provide with a new product in more detail.)

Technology, Products, and Applications Are Not Synonyms

Although many new products are not necessarily technology intensive, we will spend a few moments differentiating between technology, products, and applications. Many entrepreneurs approach prospective customers and investors with fast talk about a new product when, in fact, it is still just a technology. This section briefly covers technology-intensive products because they pose wonderful strategic opportunities as well as unique product development challenges.

A technology is a capability developed by applying specific knowledge. An example of a novel technology is PageRank, the algorithm underlying Google's AdSense product. Although other link-based ranking algorithms exist, PageRank is the most famous and supports one of the most successful companies to emerge in the last 20 years. PageRank is not for sale; the patent protecting this algorithm is owned by Stanford University. (Monetizing patents is discussed further in Chapter 5.)

PageRank (Google's trademarked name for the process) estimates a website's importance based on how many other important websites link to it, recalculating dynamically as it evaluates the entire Web. Thus, when you execute a search, you get the sites that others think are most directly relevant to your terms.

An application is the use of a capability to solve a specific problem. For instance, the PageRank algorithm is used to solve the problem of prioritizing websites relevant to a keyword or set of keywords. The difference between a technology and an application is that an application solves a problem. Interesting technologies that don't solve problems belong in science demonstration classes, not in business.

CONCEPT

Technologies and Applications
The difference between a technology and an application is that a technology applies knowledge to develop a capability, while an application solves a problem.

An application must be further developed into a product. This happens by constructing a delivery scheme and pricing structure. Thus, a product is an independently priced item that provides value to a customer.

Google's product is a subscription to AdWords, the model based on the PageRank technology. AdWords allows website owners to advertise on search result pages and pay only when someone clicks on their link. Although the algorithm is constantly being improved against spoofing schemes, it still remains one of the most powerful advertising tools in the Internet age.

Chapter 4 explains value propositions further, but Google's business model speaks to the difference between the application user and the product buyer. That is, the person using the core technology—the user conducting a search—is not the one who pays for it.

WHERE DO NEW PRODUCTS COME FROM?

Let's turn to ideas for new products. In general, product ideas are driven either by a technology or new development that pushes a product into the marketplace or by a market problem that pulls a product. In simple economic terms, this is supply- or demand-driven product design.

As we discussed earlier, a product links a capability and a solution. The step between them is a real need. Does the application address a need?

Supply-Driven Products: Hammer Meets Nail

Products often result from a new capability developed through an extensive learning or research process. In Google's case, the PageRank algorithm was developed prior to a clear market need; in the mid-1990s, people experimented with a number of search engines, and the advertising model had not yet been refined.

A supply-driven product links a capability (the ability to do something) with an application (a problem that can be solved with that capability), as shown in Figure 1-2. Products developed this way suffer from the risk that the marketplace does not have a strong need for this capability; in other words, the problem doesn't really exist. This risk is particularly high for inventors developing novel technologies. Everyone involved in marketing disruptive technologies—inventors, technology licensing agents, marketing profession-als—must be careful to address this risk from initial product development with thoughtful market analysis.

Figure 1-2   A Supply-Driven Product Links a Capability and an Application

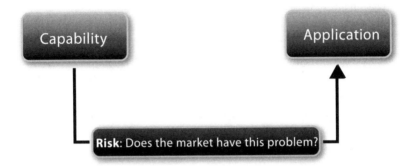

Supply-driven products may also refer to service businesses; for instance, a consultant with a strong background in operations may offer workshops on supply-chain management, enterprise software, or other items related to this background—regardless of whether the market has a need for these workshops.

This product development process is common in research organizations such as universities or government-funded laboratories. Creative research teams develop new applications before it is clear whether there is sufficient demand or whether the solution is economically feasible. In this case, institutional technology transfer offices invite investors or corporate venture groups to review their technology portfolios to look for overlap between the new application and market needs.

MINICASE

A Mouse's Tale
In his classic book, *Diffusion of Innovations*, Everett Rogers described the commercialization of the computer mouse. In 1970, when a mild recession

gripped the country, an embryonic Silicon Valley was growing near Palo Alto, and new companies were beginning to form. During this time, Douglas Engelbart invented the mouse at SRI International to control mainframe computers. Although he was not interested in controlling microcomputers this way, members of his group were; they ultimately went to the Xerox Palo Alto Research Center (PARC) and took the mouse concept with them.

However, several cultural and economic factors prevented the center from commercializing the mouse, including PARC's poor communication channels with sales groups at the Xerox parent company and that company's focus on copiers. Ultimately, Steve Jobs, cofounder of Apple Computer, visited PARC in 1979 with his engineers and saw the potential. They eventually licensed the technology and sparked a revolution with the original Macintosh computers.

As a result, even though the original mouse was developed around 1970, it did not become fully mainstream until 1984. This long penetration time is characteristic of supply-driven products with potentially interesting but immature markets; another example is the cost-effective production of microprocessors needed to power personal computers that use a mouse.

Demand-Driven Products: What I Really Want for Christmas

In general, demand-driven products are far more likely to enjoy success because companies already in the marketplace have a good understanding of the product's potential use and value. Demand-driven products connect a market problem with a solution, as shown in Figure 1-3. Demand-driven products suffer from the risk that market desire cannot be met. Christmas toys, such as Beanie Babies and Tickle Me Elmo dolls, seem to be particularly prone to this problem; just like the risk associated with supply-driven products, this risk is also met with quantitative market analysis. However, companies also face an inability to meet demand when product quality guidelines or specifications are not met. We'll discuss the implications of this problem when we talk about product recalls.

Today, many avenues connect potential product developers and markets. Satish Nambisan and Mohanbir Sawhney describe these paths in their excellent *Harvard Business Review* article, "A Buyer's Guide to the Innovation Bazaar."[3] One example is the Partners in Innovation initiative launched by Dial, the maker of Purex soap, Right Guard deodorant, and other well-known products. The company effectively ran a "beauty contest" style of competition through the United Inventors Association, paying handsome fees

Figure 1-3 A Demand-Driven Product Links a Market Problem with a Solution

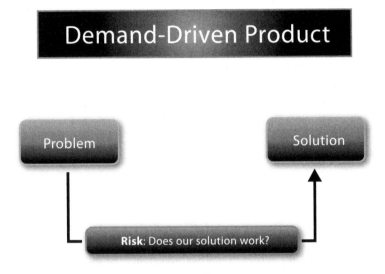

to people who had ideas that could successfully be transformed into new products.

Other companies use sites such as InnoCentive, which is similar to eBay in connecting buyers and sellers of solutions to market problems. For instance, a chemical products company might post a technical question about a specific chemical reaction. Site members can post possible solutions; the winner may earn many thousands of dollars and potentially create a long-term relationship with the buying company. This model works in today's marketplace because the Internet allows firms to reach creative people throughout the world and enables everyone to conduct rudimentary market analysis on a specific firm and its markets.

A final source of demand-driven product ideas is the so-called invention or innovation capitalists, firms that invest first in an invention or patent and then in refinements to the idea. They are basically intellectual property brokers (see Chapter 5 for more on intellectual property). Like investment banks, they are most successful when they have deep, ongoing relationships with large companies that have resources for significant sales and marketing campaigns.

Of course, it is also possible that you may develop a product idea your-self. The sprawling Gillette empire was built on a revelation by King Camp Gillette one morning while he was shaving.

MINICASE

That Was a Close One!

In his book *Cutting Edge*, Gordon McKibben describes the morning in 1895 when King Camp Gillette, shaving with the standard razor, was frustrated by its dull edge. He suddenly had an image of a razor with a disposable head and a double-sided blade. The safety razor concept took eight years to bring to maturity, but it was an instant success in the marketplace.

RISK: WHY "FASTER, BETTER, CHEAPER" DOESN'T WORK

In the 1990s, the National Aeronautics and Space Administration (NASA) adopted an exploration management philosophy dubbed "faster, better, cheaper" (FBC). In the past, the agency had followed a model featuring ex-tensively planned "flagship" missions that could take many years to realize and required budgets of approximately $1 billion. It was believed that an FBC mission would reduce budget and scope, operate on an accelerated schedule, and return successful results faster.

Unfortunately, despite some early success, the high cost of this phi-losophy became evident. First, both the Mars Climate Observer and the Mars Polar Lander missions failed in a three-month span in 1999; later, the 2003 *Columbia* tragedy that killed the entire crew was traced back to FBC. After these high-profile disasters, the agency largely abandoned FBC.

The NASA experience suggests that product and program designers must assess risk accurately and frequently. For that reason, we will spend some time on understanding sources of risk in product development. This is particularly important because introducing new products is basically a risky endeavor, and product line management and investors are fundamentally risk-averse.

Mitigating risks costs more. Therefore, each section on risk factors points out how they can be addressed.

Supply Risk

Supply risk refers to the "market pull" model described in Figure 1-3. Even if demand exists for a product, it must be manufactured and/or delivered profitably. Often product development novices talk about "making it up on volume"; however, if you lose money on each unit, you will lose lots of money on lots of units if you don't make a significant change in operations.

Risks in this category include concerns about whether your key suppliers will reliably deliver the raw materials you need. It also includes all the logistical, distribution, and operational challenges involved in delivering the product to the customer. Other factors include risks such as counterfeit manufacturing by rivals, software pirating, and other problems related to intellectual property theft.

The best way to address this risk is to ask yourself, What are the key bottlenecks? Perhaps you have good control over the way you obtain raw materials and manufacture all the components of your products because you are vertically integrated. Or you may have created your own bottlenecks and find it advantageous to outsource. You should also include macroeconomic factors like the real savings of outsourcing—changing component costs.

Supply risk applies to service businesses somewhat differently. The most common complaint of service providers is that there are not enough hours in the day—that is, you are limited by the number of hours that you can work, forcing you to turn down potential clients. This is mitigated by hiring and growing your firm; it may also be managed by raising your prices.

If you assess industry risk accurately, you can make decisions that improve your position.

MINICASE

Managing Supply Risk in the Airline Industry

Airline profits are strongly sensitive to the price of oil because it influences the cost of jet fuel. When oil prices started to rise in 2007, Southwest Airlines purchased futures contracts, effectively guaranteeing that it could buy oil in the future at a fixed price. When oil prices skyrocketed in late 2007 and early 2008, Southwest's savings were estimated at nearly $1 billion.

Economic risks such as oil prices may actually increase demand for other products. For instance, Toyota had the hybrid Prius in development long before the boom and subsequent bust of the last decade. However, when oil prices rose dramatically, Prius sales helped elevate Toyota sales over those of its American competitors.

At some level, supply risk can be mitigated with futures contracts, but if your supplier goes out of business, you may still have trouble. Effective supply chain management includes understanding the weak points in the chain and constantly monitoring them. Costs associated with mitigating supply risks include purchase prices for futures contracts and salaries related to operations management.

Demand Risk

Demand risk describes the problems inherent to the "supply-push" model shown in Figure 1-2. Are forecasts for this demand correct?

Those facing demand risk range from early-stage technology companies to independent films to sole practitioner accountants. Whenever you offer a new product to an established marketplace that has not articulated the demand, you face demand risk.

The way to mitigate this risk is to accurately evaluate demand. This is even more important than creating demand with increased marketing programs. Technology companies need to conduct market studies prior to launching a new product. Any organization should try to ramp up only at the last minute via processes like just-in-time manufacturing, where inventory levels are optimized for changing demand levels.

Just as supply risk is affected by greater economic factors, so is demand risk. In the financial crisis of 2008, many luxury goods manufacturers such as Coach and LVMH (parent of Louis Vuitton, Moet & Chandon, and other luxury brands) had to reconfigure their strategies to cope with the new environment. On the other hand, industries such as computer game developers benefited, because unemployed people at home bought more games.

MINICASE

New Coke
Coca-Cola's 1985 launch of a new formulation for its leading brand is a well-known marketing disaster. Although taste tests yielded positive results,

ultimately there was no demand for a Coke that didn't taste like Coke. The fiasco ultimately cost the company hundreds of millions of dollars in production, marketing, and launch costs.

The best way to combat this risk is to learn everything you can about your market and industry. Start with the popular business press, such as the *Wall Street Journal*, *BusinessWeek*, and *Forbes*. People engaged in business-to-business sales should read trade journals and attend trade shows to determine the key problems in the industry.

If you are engaged in market research, an Internet search can provide numbers and back up your gut instinct, but you should absolutely go out and meet your prospective customers. Listen to their needs and then meet them. There is no substitute for primary sources.

Execution Risk

Execution makes the entire product development work. Figure 1-4 shows how execution encompasses all the other sources of risk in maintaining supply and meeting demand, as well as problems that result from the link between them.

Figure 1-4   Execution Is the Process of Linking the Capability and Application with the Market Problem and Solution

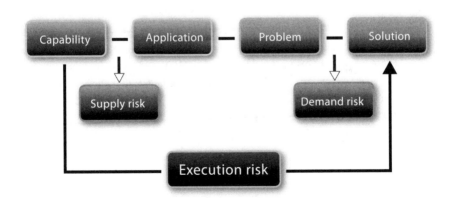

Unfortunately, there aren't many tips for mitigating execution risk, because it is hard to spend your way out of it. The best way to address it is with experience. This is why investors worry extensively about the capabilities of their firm's management team, particularly whether team members "don't know what they don't know."

It is helpful to know the roots of many execution problems. One issue is poor time management, particularly in balancing sales and production. For service providers, this is a key challenge: they are usually either getting clients or working for clients—not both simultaneously.

Another issue is planning and organization. Implementing accounting and control systems is a painful process, but it is more appealing than going out of business. Frequent review to align strategy with operations is critical. Most important, you should take feedback from your team seriously because front-line people often see the problems first. Much of this book is really a survey of common execution challenges.

MINICASE

The Newton PDA
Apple released the first personal digital assistant, the Newton, in the mid-1990s. The market apparently existed, as users flocked to the Palm Pilot five years later and made it an immediate success. Although Apple had the resources to meet the market needs, poor decisions during the design phase crippled the potential of the Newton. (Chapter 9 examines design more closely.)

HINT

Risk for Service Providers
Service providers primarily face demand risk because the costs associated with supply are so low; they have fewer issues in terms of inventory management and other processes. However, demand risk is high if a sufficient market does not exist. Execution risk is also high for service providers if they cannot manage their costs appropriately.

HINT

Risk for Entrepreneurs
Entrepreneurs face high risk in every domain. They create new markets, meaning they have high demand risk; they develop new supply chains, which means supply risk. Execution risk is particularly high because entrepreneurs who are inexperienced in management must struggle to create a corporate culture and effective communication schemes. This combination of factors helps explain why 3 out of 10 new employer firms fail in the first two years, and only half survive five years.[4]

KEYS TO SUCCESS

The keys to success at the outset are fairly simple and revolve around ruthless honesty. A product connects a capability with a solution. Do you have an application with no need or a market with no solution? Similarly, is your product defined by market pull or supply push?

Product development concerns itself with risk assessment and mitigation. Supply risk is managed with inventory control and the careful management of vendor relationships. Demand risk is managed by good market analysis and awareness of the greater economic environment. Execution is the broadest risk category and is best managed with effective controls, organization, and communication.

Service providers face different risks than manufacturers and distributors, because they take on fewer risks in capital expenditures and inventory management; in fact, for service providers, managing inventory means managing time effectively. Meanwhile, product managers and entrepreneurs differ in their resources to manage both supplier relationships and determine market demand.

The rest of this book details the product development process to show you how to mitigate these sources of risk. We will pay particular attention to the strategies used by actual companies to address these issues.

Chapter Quiz

1. Demand risk does *not* include problems of _____ .
   a. the marketplace
   b. studies of people articulating demand
   c. market size
   d. manufacturing challenges
2. Which item does *not* help mitigate execution risk?
   a. Additional funds
   b. Experience
   c. Getting team feedback
   d. Planning
3. Supply-driven products link _____ .
   a. a problem and a solution
   b. a capability and demand
   c. supply and a solution
   d. a capability and an application
4. Service providers _____ .
   a. cannot offer products because they offer services
   b. can offer products because they offer independently priced items for a set, fixed fee
   c. can only offer products purchased with services
   d. become manufacturers if they offer products
5. A product links _____ .
   a. supply and a solution
   b. a problem and demand
   c. a capability and a solution
   d. a capability and a problem
6. Innovators do *not* include which of the following?
   a. Entrepreneurs
   b. Service providers
   c. Risk avoiders
   d. Product managers
7. A technology _____ .
   a. always leads to new products
   b. solves problems without applications
   c. is the same thing as a product
   d. applies knowledge to develop a capability

8. Supply risk does *not* include problems of _____ .
   a. logistics
   b. demand
   c. operations
   d. distribution

9. Demand-driven products link _____ .
   a. a problem and a solution
   b. a problem and a capability
   c. supply and demand
   d. a capability and an application

10. Which item does *not* help service providers manage risk?
    a. Time management
    b. Better capital equipment
    c. Estimates of market demand
    d. Cost management

2

STRATEGY

If you don't know where you're going,
you might not get there.

—YOGI BERRA

Have you ever watched a house being built? First, an architect draws the plans and passes them on to the builder, who assembles the frame. Then the load-bearing walls go up, then the interior walls are erected. Eventually, the walls are painted.

This is the same process used for a new product. You draw the plans and assemble a framework before the details are worked out. Although it is possible to skip this step, and many firms actually grow without doing it effectively, the world's most successful companies take this process seriously and conduct it on a continuous basis.

What is strategy? At its best, strategy efficiently identifies opportunities that are well matched to a company's strengths and charts the path to exploiting those opportunities. Strategy also aligns overarching goals with actions. Michael Porter, arguably the world's most famous strategic thinker, has written that strategy is about making decisions. No one has the resources—time, money, or people—to pursue all paths, so strategic planning is a process of selecting the best options and discarding the rest.

Product managers must keep their corporate strategy in mind so they can align their daily activities with company resources and priorities. Frankly, this can be difficult when strategic goals seem abstract and distant in contrast with concrete, immediate problems requiring attention; but the consequences of ignoring corporate strategy are more significant in the longer term. Entrepreneurs need to be conversant with strategy because their resources are even more limited; in addition, to identify strategic partners, entrepreneurs must understand their potential partners' priorities. Finally, service providers benefit from thinking through their strategy so they can make key marketing decisions: an accountant may choose to focus on tax reporting for the garment industry, or a lawyer may specialize in estate planning for business owners. Each of these professionals needs to advertise in specific journals and prospect in different places.

CONCEPT

Strategy

Strategy efficiently identifies opportunities that are well matched to a company's strengths and charts the path to exploiting those opportunities. It also aligns overarching goals with actions.

HINT

Strategy for Service Providers

Service providers also seek opportunities matched to their strengths. For instance, during the recession, many bankruptcy lawyers increased their advertising to take advantage of the market conditions. They also hired and grew their practices to match their internal strengths to the external demand.

Although many formal theories exist for strategic formulation, this chapter introduces three popular models, each of which analyzes a different aspect of a business's interactions with the external world. Then our attention turns inward to an analysis of a company's vision and how to translate it into achievable goals. At that point, it becomes an implementation challenge when management determines daily decisions based on the firm's overall direction.

ANALYZING THE EXTERNAL ENVIRONMENT

Good strategic planning requires that you evaluate the external environment to look for opportunities. This section introduces three useful tools. First, Michael Porter's Five Forces model is useful for analyzing industries and market conditions, although this limited space cannot allow us to do justice to the entire topic. Then you will learn how to develop tables showing your strengths, weaknesses, opportunities, and threats, commonly called SWOT charts. Finally, the growth share matrix is a tool that places your product in the broader context of the market.

Porter's Five Forces

Michael Porter's seminal Five Forces model is a central concept in modern management theory. Porter determined that five forces act on any industry to determine its overall profitability and that understanding these forces as levers helps you manipulate them to your advantage.[1] We will discuss how they affect each type of innovator.

CONCEPT

Porter's Five Forces
Porter's *Five Forces* are suppliers, buyers, new entrants, substitute products, and rivalry between competitors. To understand the industry's profitability and discover opportunities, study how these forces impact your industry.

Suppliers
Suppliers are strong when there aren't many of them or when they negotiate as a group. One of Porter's examples is pilots' unions, which have strong bargaining power in the airline industry. How are you going to fly the plane without a pilot? Suppliers limit your margins by charging higher prices for their components or services.

Innovators can minimize supplier power by looking for multiple suppliers or even different sets of components. Product managers in large organizations should keep alternatives open if they are concerned about a single supplier's long-term prospects or if a supplier begins to raise prices. Entrepreneurs typically suffer more at the hands of suppliers because of the small volumes associated with early-stage companies; while strong negotiating skills help, the best way to mitigate the risk is to grow rapidly. Service providers do not usually experience many problems from suppliers because of the lack of capital goods; however, using preferred subcontractors can sometimes have similar effects if the subcontractor is "flaky" and suddenly is unable to deliver on schedule or if the relationship falters. Service providers should choose subcontractors wisely.

Of course, the flip side is that you want to be other companies' only supplier; because patents give exclusive rights to the innovator, they work well in protecting a supplier's competitive advantage (as discussed in Chapter 5). Creating relationships in which you are the preferred supplier is probably the strongest defense against this threat.

Buyers

Like suppliers, buyers have strong power when there are few of them or when they operate as a body. This is true even if the buyers are actually distributors; one example is the consumer electronics retailers who exert power because they influence consumers' decisions in stores by running promotions or allocating shelf space. Buyers limit profitability by forcing price decreases or affecting demand downstream.

Innovators can manage this risk by avoiding too much dependence on a single buyer. Product managers in large organizations typically mitigate this risk by diversifying their customer portfolios. However, even established companies may suffer from buyer threats if they are in industries with high numbers of government contracts, such as the aerospace industry, because changes in government funding priorities can force reconfiguring existing programs; in recent years, this has forced many previously successful defense and aerospace contractors to accelerate efforts to bring their technologies to the private sector. Small companies with government grants also run this risk if they do not enjoy a large portfolio of funding agencies, and thus entrepreneurs with grant funding find that they are constantly looking for money.

Even small businesses without government grants can be hurt by buyer power; many promising start-up companies have been destroyed after the elation of landing a deal with a single large buyer like Wal-Mart. Although a Wal-Mart contract typically guarantees large volumes, the retailer has been known to apply enormous pressure to reduce prices. Start-ups who cannot reduce their costs in concert find that their margins decrease rapidly or simply disappear, thus eventually forcing them out of business. Finally, service providers must always seek to diversify their client base; many a consultant has suffered from the sudden loss of a previously large contract from an established client.

New Entrants

New entrants have power if it is easy for them to replicate a specific product. Preventing this is known as creating "barriers to entry" and is done via creation of patents, strong branding, and related strategies to strengthen relationships with existing customers. For instance, a company with a patent on a new drug makes it difficult for a competitor to offer exactly the same or even a similar product, particularly because of the high investment in drug discovery. On the other hand, if you make novelty T-shirts, then the barrier to entry is low because T-shirts are commonly manufactured by many companies.

Innovators should develop intellectual property, unique distribution capabilities, or other advantages providing value that erect barriers to entry. Look to exploit new capabilities, such as improved Internet access, rather than be blindsided by them. We will talk about these advantages in later chapters on implementation.

Substitute Products

Substitute products are those that meet the same needs as existing products. If you make cookies, then your substitute threat may be candy bars, fruit (if you are talking about health-conscious consumers), or nothing (if you are trying to reach dieters). Substitutes affect your profitability because each one removes some of the demand for your product.

Substitutes pose a great threat because they are often unanticipated or they represent a complete disruption to the business model. Neighborhood travel agencies could monitor each others' performance, but they could not prevent the spread of Travelocity, Expedia, and other travel aggregators. Advertising agencies could not stop Google from revolutionizing the advertising industry with lower costs and real-time metrics (such as click-through percentages) reporting a marketing campaign's effectiveness. Service providers face the same challenges; Intuit's TurboTax products changed the accounting profession by enabling consumers to file their own tax returns at lower cost.

Innovators can defend against substitutes only by specifically identifying their added value and applying common sense to marketing decisions. Do you really want to market cookies to dieters?

Rivalry from Existing Competitors

This is easy to understand because your competitors are subject to the same forces you are. Some industries are highly competitive, such as personal computer manufacturing; think of how Hewlett-Packard, Dell, Acer, and other corporations jockey for customers. As a result, margins on computers are now less than 10 percent. On the other hand, even with stiff competition between entrenched players, some industries, like soft drink manufacturing, are still highly profitable (although that has also been due to expanding the market beyond soft drinks into bottled water, sports drinks, and other beverages).

Some rivalry actually helps because when other companies create demand, you may benefit as "a rising tide lifts all boats." Consider netbooks: the demand for cheap mininotebooks has grown as people have begun to see their value. Unfortunately, profitability drops as competition leads to price wars. (These market dynamics are discussed later in this chapter.)

Service providers are sensitive to rivalries as well; for instance, just a decade ago, the accounting profession was dominated by "The Big Eight." Today there are only four major international accounting firms. Each offers services and pricing that are approximately in line with the others; increased regulation, such as the Sarbanes-Oxley Act of 2002, has forced increased standardization of their offerings. Although the combination of standardization and regulation has contributed to a trend in elevated prices, the high prices created a gap where employees of the original eight companies could create smaller firms with slightly lower pricing attractive to midsized companies.

MINICASE

Apple's iTunes Store

In the late 1990s, a loyal base of artists and scientists valued Apple's elegant, well-designed systems, although they were a distinct minority competing against the Microsoft-controlled behemoth personal computer market. Meanwhile, the music industry was in a confusing transition to the digital age as peer-to-peer music sharing services effectively created institutional music piracy. Prior to the digital revolution, music publishers held great power because a small number of studios provided all the content; the future now looked hazy and threatening to the studios.

Apple saw that with the onset of digital downloads, buyers held tremendous power in the music industry and had basically negotiated free music; this was accelerated by the rivalry between competitors that prevented studios from creating platforms on which other publishers' work might appear. By stepping into the void as a publisher-agnostic distribution channel, Apple was able to exploit all these transformations. None of the studios had seen a computer manufacturer as a rival or had foreseen how the iTunes Store would transform the music industry.

Searching for Blue Oceans

In their 2005 breakout book, W. Chan Kim and Renée Marbourgne developed an alternative way of thinking about strategy.[2] They argued that instead of looking at existing industry structures, a company can instead create an entirely different framework, moving from the bloody red oceans of established cutthroat competition to uncontested blue oceans. Creating a "blue ocean strategy" has six key principles:

Reconstruct Market Boundaries

Reconstructing market boundaries calls for understanding current divisions in an existing marketplace and offering new products at the interfaces. Kim and Mauborgne describe how the women's fitness franchise Curves redefined the gym marketplace. Previously, women worked out at gyms with high membership fees and many amenities, where they often felt self-conscious in an environment filled with mirrors and competitive men; or they worked out at home with videotapes, where they were both lonely and easily distracted. Curves offered a no-frills, low-cost gym with affordable membership fees to bring women out of the home and into a comfortable, sharing environment.

Focus on the Big Vision

Staying focused on the big vision allows you to create a product with consistent value and thus a consistent story; visualizing it often highlights areas where you cannot reconcile elements of your strategy. Consider how irritated we get when we have to wait for fast food. The "wait" and "fast food" represent inherent contradictions; we are willing to wait at a restaurant but not at a fast food joint. I'll talk more about ensuring that you offer features that provide benefits in Chapter 4.

Reach Beyond Existing Demand

You can grow by offering more to your existing customers or by signing on new customers. If you wish to enlist new clientele, you must understand why they have not previously signed on. Have they rejected your offering or are they simply unexposed to your product? Turning these groups into customers requires different sales strategies. For instance, most major fast-food chains offer salads to convert potential customers who reject the original core offerings for health concerns. In addition, these companies continue to open locations around the world, penetrating previously inaccessible markets. Traditional fast-food restaurants pursuing these two paths thus reach out to previously rejecting customers as well as to unexposed ones.

Analyze the Strategic Sequence
Analyzing the strategic sequence calls for ensuring that there is demand and room to differentiate your product *before* you analyze your product's potential for profitability. A low-cost strategy is only low cost if the price supports a margin. In other words, no matter how cheaply you can make a buggy whip, it is just not cheap enough. A market study is critical to this strategic effort.

Overcome Organizational Roadblocks
Understand your organization's bottlenecks and learn how to work around them. Kim and Mauborgne give the interesting example of William Bratton's leadership of the New York Police Department in the 1990s. Bratton desperately needed more staff but faced severe budget limitations. He discovered that locations reporting frequent crime and safer areas were staffed equally. On the other hand, officers lost tremendous amounts of time processing criminals in court (the average was sixteen hours). Therefore, Bratton created "bust buses"—old buses retrofitted into mobile police stations that could be moved to crime-heavy locations, processing criminals on the spot in just an hour. This solved both the loss of manpower during criminal processing and increased the police presence in crime-heavy locations.

Incorporate Execution into Strategy
Effective product development requires creating buy-in at every level of the organization. I will talk more about Nordstrom's management style in Chapter 7, but the company's strategy of offering quality products with top-notch customer service is well-known. To execute this strategy, however, it is obviously insufficient for the CEO to say, "We will provide excellent service" without teaching this philosophy to the salespeople. Any organization that hopes to develop fans in its customer base needs to develop internal fans first.

Be a SWOT Team

Another useful tool for analysis is to analyze your company's strengths, weaknesses, opportunities, and threats (SWOT). While the Porter formalism focuses on competitive forces driving profitability, SWOT analysis reveals internal company dynamics in the strengths and weaknesses sections and external forces under opportunities and threats. SWOT analysis is often presented in a grid, as shown in Figure 2-1.

Figure 2-1   An Example of SWOT Analysis

Strengths

- Organizational capabilities
- Processes we excel at
- Protected intellectual property
- Brand
- Customer relationships
- Management experience

Weaknesses

- Missing capabilities
- Inefficient processes
- Ways we cannot compete
- Poor customer experiences
- Gaps in management skill sets

Opportunities

- Changes in marketplace
- Improved cost structures
- Government regulation favoring our product

Threats

- New competition
- Increased cost
- Problematic regulation

CONCEPT

SWOT Analysis

SWOT analysis characterizes a company's strengths, weaknesses, opportunities, and threats. The goal is to match opportunities with strengths and identify ways to mitigate weaknesses and external threats.

SWOT analysis uncovers opportunities that correlate to the company's strengths. This analysis is most effective when management practices ruthless honesty about its weaknesses and its ability to respond to changes in the external environment.

Internal items typically sorted into strengths and weaknesses include management of customer relationships, specific manufacturing capabilities, the strength of the corporate culture, and brand quality. Additional corporate characteristics include management deficiencies—for instance, a retiring vice president for marketing might present a sudden weakness in the organization.

Opportunities and threats describe the external environment. Changing market conditions might consist of demographic transitions, such as the retirement of baby boomers or changing immigrant populations. Additional factors include the overall economy, regulatory changes, and other large-scale movements.

MINICASE

P&G Adjacencies

Procter & Gamble (P&G) practices a strategy of "adjacencies," in which the company develops products that exploit one of its existing brands in a given market segment.[3] For instance, P&G's moves in the oral care segment have exploited the company's strengths in brand equity and market position to create and seize new opportunities. The company has leveraged the Crest brand to expand beyond toothpaste into whitening strips, flosses, and power toothbrushes. This line grew both through internally developed products and through acquisition.

SWOT analysis provides different information than the Porter Five Forces model. Porter's model analyzes the industry as a whole, whereas SWOT matches industry opportunities to the company's strengths.

Growth Share Matrix

Another tool in the strategist's box is the use of the growth share matrix, also known as the "BCG matrix" for Boston Consulting Group, which originally developed and popularized it. The basic two-by-two matrix plots market growth rate vertically and market share horizontally. The market is then divided into four quadrants, as shown in Figure 2-2. By placing your product concept in the appropriate sector, you can determine if your product is attractive from the company's perspective. (Attractiveness from the customer's perspective is described more fully Chapter 4.) The four sectors are:

Figure 2-2   An Example of the Growth Share Matrix

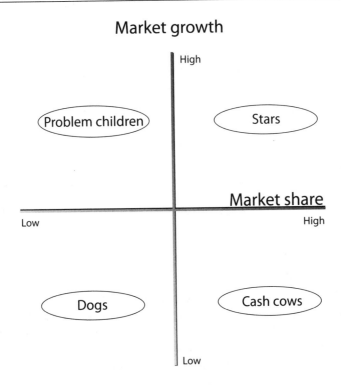

1. **Dogs:** These products have a small market share in slowly growing markets. Examples might include businesses selling pay phones (don't laugh—this came up in a recent California election); pay phones became much less interesting when cell phones became popular 10 years ago. Products for low growth rate markets with small market shares need to be extremely profitable to make them worthwhile, and such high profits are difficult to find in a market without much activity.

2. **Cash cows:** These products control a large share of a relatively flat market. This is the problem faced by managers of Procter & Gamble, Johnson & Johnson, and other consumer product companies in established markets. Products may generate decent profits, and their enormous volume maintains the appeal. Slowly growing markets make these markets less "sexy," but they can be effective engines for ongoing profits; in essence, they provide rather predictable returns for low risk.

3. **Stars:** These businesses enjoy high market share in a rapidly growing arena; Netscape and Google grew in this fashion. Although Google has developed an enormous portfolio of auxiliary product lines, none has enjoyed the stellar success of the original AdSense and AdWords programs, which puts the company in danger of becoming an enormous one-trick pony.

4. **Problem children:** Businesses or products in these markets can be troubling because they consume significant marketing dollars to keep up with the high growth, but presumably fierce competition keeps the market share low. These products drain resources and attention. The best solution here is to use marketing dollars extremely wisely and consider strategic alliances early.

CONCEPT

Growth Share Matrix

The *growth share matrix* approach analyzes the market potential of various product opportunities.

From a product development perspective, it is usually better to have high market shares, whether from exciting, rapidly growing markets or from slow-growing ones. This is the philosophy that keeps Kraft, Procter & Gamble, and many other large corporations seeking new products; if they already have high market share in relatively similar market segments, then it is easier to tune up the machine to market a new product and enjoy high market share again.

Of course, if you are trying to enter a new market, by definition, you have a low market share. This is the dilemma faced by start-up companies and companies trying to expand past their current customer base. As described in the classic book *Positioning: The Battle for Your Mind* by Al Ries and Jack Trout, it is best to define your market so you are the leader and then expand the boundaries of that market. In this way, you maintain and exploit the benefits of having high market share.

MINICASE

GE Reverse Innovation

General Electric (GE) has developed a new "reverse innovation" strategy.[4] In the early 2000s, the company sought to accelerate its internal growth to minimize dependence on acquisitions; management also sought to fuel fast growth by growing in emerging markets. This reverse innovation strategy called for developing novel technology products with reasonable performance at low costs: "a 50 percent solution at a 15 percent price."

In China, the company generated a stunning success with its portable ultrasound machines. Because more than 90 percent of the population relies on low-tech hospitals or basic clinics without imaging centers, no market existed for the high-performance machines commonly used in the United States and Europe. So GE developed a revolutionary compact ultrasound that ran off a standard laptop and sold for as little as $15,000—less than 15 percent of the price of the high-end machines. The laptop-based design made it possible to fine-tune the applications after the machines were purchased. After six years, the product was a $278 million global product line for GE.

ANALYZING INTERNAL DIRECTION

So far we have discussed ways to analyze external forces and opportunities. How do you account for company culture and dreams? A separate formula describes internal strategic planning.

Although strategic theory teems with buzzwords, you must learn how to think about your company's general goals and then narrow them down to make daily decisions. (To entertain yourself, look on the Internet for mission statement generators. They typically combine words such as *focus*, *customer*, *discipline*, and *experience* in random order to generate a new statement.)

Vision and Mission

Start by articulating "what you want to be when you grow up," or your vision. Often these statements include phrases like "We aspire to be . . ." or "We aim to . . ." In contrast, a mission statement describes your company's values. Many firms combine these statements into general philosophies or just call them "the company way" if they embody a number of principles.

Let's look at some examples to see how vision and mission statements guide product development efforts because the company's mission states how customers should expect to find value. Consider Wal-Mart: "Wal-Mart's mission is to help people save money so they can live better." This is clearly not the home of glitzy products presented by elegant sales professionals. However, this mission makes modern cost-cutting, logistical solutions interesting to management.

On the other hand, chemical giant DuPont says, "Founded in 1802, DuPont puts science to work by creating sustainable solutions essential to a better, safer, healthier life for people everywhere." While Wal-Mart's mission emphasizes offering low-cost products, DuPont's mission statement focuses on "better" and "sustainable" solutions. Therefore, you would not expect for DuPont's products to be the cheapest in the marketplace, but you would expect for the company to uphold a higher environmental standard.

One company that can tell you its reason for being is telecommunications giant AT&T: "Today, our mission is to connect people with their world, everywhere they live and work, and do it better than anyone else. We're fulfilling this vision by creating new solutions for consumers and businesses and by driving innovation in the communications and entertainment industry." This explains why the same company provides many people's pay-per-view movies, phone service, and Internet access. It connects them with the world around them.

This catalog shows us two things: (1) the vision and mission statement may not be clearly separated for every company, but global giants tend to clearly articulate global visions; and (2) whether it is a vision, mission, philosophy, or values statement, general "Why we are here" statements effectively set the tone for the direction of a company's growth.

Goals and Objectives

Imagine that you have a mission to be "the world's most respected provider of widgets." How does this impact your widget-buying customers? How does your vice president of marketing select the right trade journal in which to advertise? In other words, if strategy is about identifying opportunities and making decisions, how do you move from grandiose goals to daily decision making?

The link is through goals and objectives. Each of these steps operates as a zoom lens, clarifying how to realize a vision through a series of well-considered steps. Unlike your mission and vision, your goals and objectives will change over time as you reassess your progress.

In that case, why do organizations create new mission statements? This usually happens when the organization doesn't fully understand its own culture. Hewlett-Packard's underlying principles reflect the values of its founders: high respect for employees, quality and reliability in products, and participation in the community's well-being. The company honored these priorities in fact, if not on paper, long before it was codified as the HP Way, and thus the mission has remained essentially unchanged since the company's founding in 1939. Companies that frequently rewrite their mission and vision statements demonstrate that they don't understand their internal principles or their products' value to their customers. A consistent vision leads to consistent value in the marketplace.

Although the terms are often used interchangeably, in formal strategic theory *goals* indicate intentions, while *objectives* are quantifiable. Goals identify specific targets. Unlike the mission and vision, goals are constantly reevaluated. They also lead to quantifiable measures of success.

As an innovator of computer games, for instance, your goal might be "To sell to young computer gamers." The associated objective would then be "To sell 10,000 units to computer gamers under age 25."

Goals and objectives can quantify your progress in units, dollars, profit, or any other metric. It is important to put something down on paper, though, so you can track your progress in a measurable way. "Doing better with our present customers" is vague and will not help you achieve your goals.

Internal Strategic Elements

A company's *vision* describes where it wants to be in the future, while its *mission* identifies its core values. In many corporate values statements, the vision and mission are combined. If you are an entrepreneur, it is especially important to ensure that your new product and its market are aligned with your corporate values. The next step is to identify *goals*, or intentions, and then meet them through quantifiable *objectives*.

Maximizing Profitability

Now that you have analyzed your industry and your company, you have some idea of the most appealing paths for your new product. As stated at the beginning of this chapter, strategy primarily provides tools for making decisions. How does that work after you have generated pages of analytical results? What benchmarks do you use to determine which path is best?

Porter has written extensively that the goal of strategic planning exercises should be to maximize profitability. Profitability is approximately the product of the margin and the volume, where the margin is the profit on each item and the volume is the total number of items sold.

Business management is often a balance between margin and volume. As the margin increases, fewer customers can afford you; as it decreases, more customers sign up, as illustrated in Figure 2-3. Of course, the ideal scenario is one where both these terms increase—but in an open economy, someone is bound to notice, so competition appears and the price (margin) begins to decrease.

Maximizing Profitability

Profitability is roughly defined as margin multiplied by volume. Usually one increases at the expense of the other. When both increase, competition usually appears and drives the price back down. Strategy concerns itself with maximizing profitability.

Figure 2-3   The Customer Volumes Decrease as Price and Margin Increase

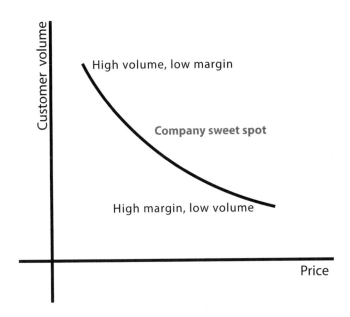

Service providers perform the same balancing act as they define their hourly rate (note that this is not recommended as the best pricing strategy). A low rate may bring in more clients, but a higher rate generates more profit per hour. Each provider must decide which path makes more sense to realize his mission.

Generic Market Strategies

Porter has also written quite a bit about the three generic strategies available to maintain an advantage in the marketplace. One option is to take a large market and segment it somehow, then focus your attention on one of those segments. However, to approach a broad market, two other strategies—representing two extremes—are also possible: cost leadership and differentiation.

You can understand these latter strategies intuitively by thinking about what may be called the "Wal-Mart/Nordstrom dilemma." Wal-Mart has become one of the world's largest companies by driving down prices in almost any field it enters—grocery, furniture, consumer electronics, and so on. Its profits come from making a slender margin on millions of customers every day. On the other hand, Nordstrom performs well by maximizing its value to the customer but at higher prices. Its margins on a single sale may be higher than Wal-Mart's, but fewer customers can afford to shop there.

Answering the Wal-Mart/Nordstrom dilemma for yourself is a major philosophical decision. Are you about volume or margin? How do you implement this in your hiring decisions, vendor management, or marketing budget?

As Wal-Mart notes on its website, the company operates more than 40 regional distribution centers, each of which exceeds one million square feet in size, operates 24/7, and has more than five miles of conveyor belt. Each of these centers clearly represents a major investment in infrastructure. Meanwhile, the company does not invest as heavily in personnel; PBS reports that employees' average weekly take-home pay is $250.

On the other hand, Nordstrom's invests more in its sales force; the hourly salesperson earns an average salary of $34,500,[5] including a commission that varies by department.[6] At 52 weeks per year and a 15 percent tax bracket, that works out to a weekly take-home pay of about $563, or more than double the Wal-Mart salary. This difference likely results from a combination of commission and the number of hours worked; both represent investments in people because the commission motivates better performance, while hourly salespeople typically seek to work more hours. This pays off in turnover as well; reportedly 70 percent of Wal-Mart employees leave within the first year,[7] while Nordstrom's turnover is a remarkably low 25 percent.[8]

In short, Wal-Mart's commitment to low-cost products led to increased investment in infrastructure, while Nordstrom's focus on service suggested allocating resources to retaining the sales force. Clearly articulating a company's strategy helps management identify its top priorities and focus resources accordingly.

CONCEPT

Generic Market Strategies

For broad markets, the general strategies available boil down to *cost leadership* and *differentiation*. A third strategy is to *segment the market* and focus specifically on the needs of one or more segments.

Value Innovation

Just as Kim and Marbourgne develop strategic analysis tools in contrast to Porter's industry analysis, they also argue that a company can simultaneously seek lowered cost structure and differentiation in pursuit of what they call "value innovation." Value innovation calls for discarding cost elements representing traditional competitive features and replacing them with new elements unmatched by other industry players. To pursue value innovation, you must fully understand the value offered by each cost element.

One way to look at value innovation is to search for opportunities to create hybrids from different industries. For instance, you might describe Google as "the Yellow Pages meets commercials," offering the easy search of the Yellow Pages with the advertising sophistication of a commercial. The gaming industry has thrived by offering the diversity of arcades with the ability to keep your teenager at home.

MINICASE

Cirque du Soleil

Kim and Marbourgne describe how Cirque du Soleil captures value innovation. Consider how circuses suffered with growing audience discomfort with animal performances, as well as from high costs commensurate with entertaining in three rings. The circus experience was geared toward children. On the other hand, high-end theaters offered intimate venues with sophisticated stories, commanding higher ticket prices in the process. Cirque du Soleil therefore discarded the expensive animal acts, reduced the staff requirements by offering a single "ring" at a time, and presented an elegant show in a sophisticated venue. The founders of Cirque du Soleil created an entirely new circus-theater hybrid.

CONCEPT

Value Innovation

Value innovation calls for simultaneous pursuit of lowered cost structure and differentiation by seeking to eliminate traditional competitive industry elements and introducing new advantages without competition in the marketplace.

KEYS TO SUCCESS

Product development strategy is the process by which you search for opportunities, then design a concrete plan to exploit them. Strategic planning can be an abstract exercise or a weekend workshop; but in quality organizations, it is a continuous activity. Certainly successful solo practitioners conduct this activity almost on a daily basis, while large organizations typically have teams that meet frequently to look for opportunities and respond to the changing environment.

Several tools exist for analyzing the external environment. Michael Porter's Five Forces model provides a look at the profit levers in an entire industry and allows you to take advantage of internal strengths and environmental weaknesses, while a "blue ocean" analysis identifies opportunities to profitably disrupt an existing industry structure. A SWOT analysis indicates how to match your company's strengths to available external opportunities in order to increase both sales and profitability. Finally, a growth share matrix allows you to place your current product portfolio and those of your competitors in the context of the marketplace.

Once you identify external opportunities, you need to conduct an internal analysis to find the ways in which your corporate strengths are well-suited to meeting marketplace needs. Clearly articulating your vision and mission will show you where you are going and why. Then you can establish your goals and objectives to quantify how you will measure success. This way, you can take the needed steps to ensure that you meet your objectives. Your goals and objectives should all generally lead to maximizing your profitability. You can then select the generic market strategy—cost leadership, differentiation, or market segmentation—that best aligns with your vision and the external environment, or perhaps pursue a value innovation strategy simultaneously combining cost leadership and differentiation.

All of these abstractions guarantee that as you mature your product, you can optimize your company's resources and shore up weaknesses when necessary. They also guarantee that you are paying attention to changes in the external environment and responding appropriately.

Before you write strategy and planning off as a silly exercise, consider a Japanese proverb: "Vision without action is a daydream. Action without vision is a nightmare."

Chapter Quiz

1. Profitability is approximately the product of _____ .
   a. margin and volume
   b. margin and demand
   c. supply and volume
   d. price and margin

2. Strategy does all of the following except _____ .
   a. identify opportunities matched to company strengths
   b. chart the path to exploiting opportunities
   c. align goals and actions
   d. create additional jobs for management

3. Objectives must be _____ .
   a. qualitative
   b. easily met
   c. ambitious
   d. quantifiable

4. Which of the following is *not* one of Porter's Five Forces?
   a. Substitutes
   b. New entrants
   c. Government
   d. Buyers

5. Which of the following is *not* an internal strategic element?
   a. Goals
   b. Mission
   c. Market
   d. Vision

6. All of the following are common tools for analyzing strategies except _____ .
   a. enterprise resource analysis
   b. growth share matrix
   c. Porter's Five Forces model
   d. SWOT analysis

7. Which of the following is *not* one of Porter's generic market strategies?
   a. Differentiation
   b. Demand analysis
   c. Market segmentation
   d. Cost leadership

8. The growth share matrix analyzes _____ .
   a. management strength
   b. supply risk
   c. market opportunities
   d. innovation quality

9. The corporate mission identifies _____ .
   a. the market of interest
   b. the company's core values
   c. the company's product line
   d. management's objectives

10. Which of the following is *not* part of SWOT analysis?
    a. Supply
    b. Weaknesses
    c. Opportunities
    d. Threats

3

MARKETING

Customers buy for their reasons, not yours.
—ORVEL RAY WILSON

I n business school, I dreaded my marketing class, fearing it would be about graphic design; this misconception came from watching too many episodes of Donald Trump's reality show "The Apprentice." Fortunately, Professor Dave McMahon set me straight; I hope I can do justice to his insights.

Modern marketing theory was born in the advertising heyday of the 1950s, when overproduction motivated management to convince consumers to buy things they "didn't know they needed." As today's business management theories and practice began taking shape, experts started thinking of all aspects of the business as elements of the "marketing machine."

Successful product development requires that you think through marketing before you complete your product design and look at every element as a chance to communicate your value.

DEFINITION OF MARKETING

Harvard Business School professor Theodore Levitt defined marketing as "the process of creating, satisfying, and retaining customers." This broad definition includes most aspects of the business process:

- Creating customers refers to creating and communicating the value proposition (defined in Chapter 4), identifying prospective customers, and generating a transaction.
- Satisfying customers describes delivery of the product and meeting all transaction terms.
- Retaining customers signifies communicating ongoing value to generate additional transactions.

CONCEPT

Marketing

Marketing is the process of creating, satisfying, and retaining customers.

THE DIFFERENCE BETWEEN SALES AND MARKETING

We might also call this discussion "how to succeed in marketing without being a used car salesman." Many people associate marketing with sales activities, when, in fact, sales is but a small part of the process. Levitt defined sales as the communication process to generate a transaction, making it a key element of but not the same thing as marketing.

This definition of marketing holds for service providers as well, which is why it is difficult for solo practitioners to grow their businesses; it is nearly impossible to generate new business (create customers) while completing assignments for existing clients (satisfying customers). For this reason, combining these activities is critical.

NUMBERS, NUMBERS, NUMBERS

Marketing embodies both strategy and tactics. Most of all, it is a highly analytical discipline. Because you can't know in advance which programs will be most effective, true marketing gurus quantify relentlessly.

Even though they are both quantitative disciplines, marketing and engineering still do not work together well in many organizations, creating a stumbling block. Engineers assess a product's performance using a number of easily quantified and verified tests and measurements. On the other hand, while marketing is also highly analytical and quantified, many assumptions underlying a marketing plan cannot be verified easily. How many customers will we lose with a price that is 10 percent higher? We don't know. Will people sign up in three months or in six months? We don't know. (I have frequently told my clients that the one set of numbers that will be absolutely wrong is the set in the business plan.)

The Internet has transformed how we do business and enables rapid progress through the segmentation, targeting, positioning process (described next) and assessment. This provides some comfort to engineers, but everyone still has to come to terms with the fundamental "guesstimate" nature of true marketing.

SEGMENTATION, TARGETING, POSITIONING

The segmentation, targeting, positioning (STP) process takes place early in the product development cycle and helps you identify, select, and approach your target customers.[1] This turns your marketing campaign into a "rifle-shot" instead of a novice "shotgun" approach.

CONCEPT

Segmentation, Targeting, Positioning

The *segmentation, targeting, positioning (STP)* process takes place early in the product development cycle and helps you identify, select, and approach your target customers. *Segmentation* is the process of dividing your potential customer base into groups with similar needs. *Targeting* is the selection of one or more of these segments as your prospects. *Positioning* is understanding and manipulating your prospect's perception of your product.

Segmentation

Segmentation is the process of dividing your potential customer base into groups with similar needs, under the theory that they will likely respond in similar ways to how those needs are addressed. Common segmentation schemes include the following:

- **Geographic:** Geographic segmentation divides your customer base by country, community, or some other regional unit. This is more important than ever for manufacturing operations because of today's improved access to emerging economies. Service providers often segment this way by default because they reach their clients through building one-on-one relationships.
- **Psychographic:** Psychographic segmentation analyzes your customer base by personality or character traits. This is far more critical in consumer marketing than in business-to-business outreach, particularly when seeking so-called early adopters who will market on your behalf. Everett Rodgers's *Diffusion of Innovations* and Malcolm Gladwell's more recent *The Tipping Point* describe how some people accelerate social word-of-mouth phenomena; searching for these influencers is a key use of psychographic segmentation.
- **Demographic:** Demographic analysis divides your potential customer base by age, gender, race, social class, or other group characteristics.
- **Behavioral:** Behavior segmentation analyzes your customers in terms of actions they do in a similar fashion. For instance, you might advertise differently to repeat customers versus new ones.

Business-to-business innovators may segment their target companies by the organization instead of by individuals, using metrics such as these:

- **Geographic:** Businesses commonly serve other organizations in a specific region.
- **Organization type:** Some people do brisk business with public agencies, while others only sell to privately held companies. Another way to sort prospective customers is by role (manufacturers, distributors, and so on).
- **Industry focus:** This is particularly effective for service providers, such as accountants who focus on nursing homes or bankers who concentrate on technology companies.

MINICASE

Climbing the Ladder of Success

General Motors was famous in the 1950s and 1960s for segmenting its market economically and offering a product "ladder" with products designed for various income levels. Customers "entered" at Chevrolet and then traded up to Pontiac, Oldsmobile, Buick, and Cadillac;[2] an extensive advertising campaign effectively communicated the ladder's steps to prospective customers (as well as to everyone else, so that the unwritten code was clear to those the customer was trying to impress). This model lasted for 40 years, until foreign brands and a major recession forced the American auto industry to restructure. At that point it became clear that the brands' distinction was meaningless to entire generations of buyers, with only the "Cadillac" connotations remaining (although one might argue that the low extreme, the Chevy, also is firmly ingrained in our consciousness).

Targeting

Targeting is the selection of potential prospects based on your segmentation scheme. For instance, if you sell boys' underwear, you are unlikely to be as concerned with segmenting the United States geographically as you are with reaching moms.

As Philip Kotler and Kevin Lane Keller explain in their classic *Marketing Management* that segmentation only works if the segments look good for five criteria:

- **Differentiable:** They must respond differently to various communication schemes. Otherwise there is no point in segmenting them; why would an entrepreneur develop different computer accessories for women and men if they are not going to respond differently?
- **Measurable:** You must be able to quantify the segment size, growth rate, and purchasing power of each segment so you can measure your progress in reaching your targets.
- **Substantial:** The market must be large enough that it is worthwhile to scale your operation. Service providers often reach out opportunistically instead of focusing on large markets.

- **Accessible:** You must be able to reach these markets. A Nebraska company focused on serving hair salons in Paris may struggle.
- **Actionable:** It must be possible to reach targets with specific marketing programs. This has been an ongoing challenge for companies trying to reach emerging economies that use different communication methods than industrialized nations (such as fewer magazines or greater use of cell phones).

MINICASE

Saturday Morning Cartoons
The commercials that are run during cartoon programs advertise toys because the manufacturers are targeting children. This speaks to changes in family buying habits; even without their own salaries, children control ever-larger portions of discretionary income.

Positioning

Positioning is based on the simple belief that the key to marketing lies in understanding and manipulating your prospect's perception of your product. The classic book *Positioning: The Battle for Your Mind* by Al Ries and Jack Trout describes methods to create your position. The basic steps are as follows:

1. **Determine your current position and that of your competitors in the marketplace.** Use focus groups, surveys, or other tools to look at your current position. Entrepreneurs have an opportunity to create a new position, but they almost always land at the "you won't get fired for buying IBM" syndrome, where customers fear buying from someone new without an established reputation. Thus they need extra creativity to break through a target's skepticism.
2. **Define your goal.** Typically you will want to position your product as the leader in the marketplace, but with some freedom in defining the "marketplace." This goal should align with your market segmentation strategy.
3. **Create a plan.** Ries and Trout have described the most effective strategies for various positions (leader, follower) and situations (line

extensions, fighting major competitors). These communication techniques describe how to create finely tuned messages, whether it is to defend your good position or change a poor one. You can also communicate placement in the marketplace with direct tools, such as elaborating on points of parity and points of difference with competitors and other players in the landscape.

4. **Measure and reassess.** The key to any marketing program is to continue to take the pulse of your place in the market. Today it is easier than ever to gauge consumer response via the Internet; business-to-business innovators can also assess their position via simple surveys. Nothing, however, takes the place of good listening to clients and prospects.

MINICASE

The Olympics

The Olympics are the world's preeminent sporting tournament. Some new sports, such as snowboarding, are perceived as legitimate only when they are included in the Olympic games. As a result, leaders of these new activities conduct lengthy campaigns to qualify as Olympics events so they will benefit by association.

Perspective on STP

As we discussed in Chapter 2, the two key activities of strategy development are to identify opportunities and make decisions. The STP process is absolutely central to these two pursuits. No matter how large or well-funded you are, you still have to allocate your resources wisely. Thinking through this process early in product development will save you agony later.

If you follow the steps in the STP process as part of your strategic planning, they will help you identify and reach your prospects and then articulate your value to them.

MARKETING FOUR Ps

Once you have identified your target market, you must decide what you are offering them and communicate this to your prospects. The Four Ps, originally defined by Jerome McCarthy as the classic "marketing mix," characterize all the tools at your disposal to reach, satisfy, and retain your customers. They are commonly defined as follows:[3]

- **Product:** features, specifications, and supporting warranties and guarantees
- **Price:** economics, including discounts and time and energy costs
- **Place:** distribution methods, geography, and segmentation
- **Promotion:** advertising, publicity, sales promotions, and branding

CONCEPT

The Four Ps

McCarthy's classic marketing mix, the *Four Ps*, consists of product, price, place, and promotion. *Product* describes features, specifications, and supporting warranties and guarantees. *Price* represents the product economics, including discounts and payment terms, as well as time and energy costs. *Place* comprises all processes involved in getting the product to the customer and any related market segmentation. Finally, *promotion* describes all elements of advertising, public relations, and branding.

Product

Product includes the features and specifications, as well as the supporting warranties and guarantees. Innovators typically think through the features first because they have a sense of what the product should do, but visionaries struggle with detailed specifications. Even service providers need to think through project requirements; "mission creep," where the work balloons outside the scope laid out originally at the project's inception, is a common complaint for those who have not thoroughly defined and limited the scope of work they can/will do.

Warranties and guarantees are equally important. They assure the customer that the product is sold in good faith and that the company values the customer relationship more than the transaction. Manufacturing innovators must design and implement a quality control process. This may mean reducing the initial breadth of the product line to maintain quality and evaluate user feedback prior to branching out.

Licensed service providers such as accountants and lawyers offer implied guarantees through the certification process; however, consultants run the risk of appearing to sell services without any guarantees. It is therefore more important to write a clear scope of work and metrics for success in the engagement agreement. Alan Weiss has written extensively and clearly on this topic.

MINICASE

L.L.Bean's Guarantees and Branding

The retailer L.L.Bean offers a lifetime guarantee on its products; in fact, the company's slogan is "Guaranteed. You have our word." The page on its website that shows this guarantee also has an image of a sign from the original store's wall dating from 1916. It says, "I do not consider a sale complete until goods are worn out and customer still satisfied."

Price

Price refers to the economics of the product purchase, including discounts and payment terms. Furthermore, it includes additional time and energy costs paid by the consumer. The customer obviously will not buy your product if it is not priced favorably.

Today's consumer expects to have a shorter learning curve than in the past. Early personal computers did not color-code the ports for the mouse, keyboard, and other accessories, requiring a near-expert to assemble the system; in later years, the use of color coding increased as sales expanded beyond computer-savvy techs to "regular people."

Plug-and-play originally referred to computer accessories but now describes general relationships. Today's customers—whether in business-to-business or business-to-consumer situations—expect to be able to use new products easily and will not tolerate extensive training programs.

MINICASE

What Items Really Cost

In a *Harvard Business Review* article, Richard Wise and Peter Baumgartner describe how the final price of many items, such as computers and cars, is as much as five times the original item price when financing, service, technical support, and other charges are taken into account.[4]

Place

Place includes any process involved in getting the product to the customer. It may also refer to market segmentation, such as geographic or demographic factors, that change the method of product delivery or communications.

Consider Intuit, maker of popular financial management software packages like Quicken and QuickBooks. You can buy the company's products from retail office supply stores, including Staples, OfficeMax, and Office Depot; websites for those stores and other discount suppliers; and directly from the Intuit website. Prior to the widespread use of the Internet, Intuit could only reach its customers through retail stores, but now that new online channels are available, the company has an entirely new way to reach people and build ongoing relationships. However, Intuit had to learn how to interact directly with its ultimate customers—a challenge it had not faced previously. We will discuss this in more detail in Chapter 10.

Segmentation is related to place because different customers buy in different ways. A lawyer who is used to finding clients through her network might find people with different types of cases if she attracts them on a website or via articles published in trade journals.

MINICASE

The Online World

Today many manufacturers realize significantly higher margins by selling through online marketplaces such as eBay, Amazon, and their own websites. Direct marketing to create this channel may be a bigger investment than selling through distributors, but it can ultimately be more profitable. It is important to consider the relative profit potential of different distribution strategies.

Promotion

Promotion is the element that most often comes to mind when people think of marketing. Promotion includes all elements of advertising, public relations, and branding.

Today every communication must be considered an opportunity for promotion. Even your invoices give you a chance to reinforce your brand. Beware, though, since self-promotion has saturated every aspect of our society. You can rise above it with verifiable third-party reviews when possible, but avoid testimonials from "Anne M." or similar cop-outs.

A special category of promotion is viral marketing, or using existing networks to broadcast your brand. Social networking sites fall into this category, as do other mechanisms that have others point to your product, such as links on related websites. Manage these communication channels carefully, because this is still a rapidly changing, dynamic field—although there is plenty of room for experimentation.

MINICASE

Viral Marketing

The classic example of viral marketing is Hotmail, one of the first free e-mail services. Hotmail automatically appended its advertising to outgoing e-mails from its users, thus generating more advertising from each use.

Perspective on the Four Ps

Innovators need to remember the Four Ps of marketing for product development, which apply not only to products, but to any communication program in which you are trying to create a new behavior.

If you are an entrepreneur, think about the Four Ps when you raise capital with the mind-set of marketing your company. You can give the equivalent of warranties and guarantees by offering good governance. The price of your deal is the stock price or interest rate on your note, including all the deal terms. Place includes the methods you use to find investors: are you submitting your business plan anonymously or reaching out to find investors face-to-face? Promotion and branding applies to deals as much as to products; in an active investment community, some deals generate significant buzz and are funded quickly and at more favorable terms to the entrepreneur.

HINT

The Four Ps for Service Providers

Service providers also need to face the Four Ps. In addition to offering new services (products) and setting fees (price), lawyers, accountants, bankers, consultants, and many others tend to struggle with place and promotions. They tend to market in a rather haphazard manner instead of effectively reaching out to new clients and spreading a consistent brand.

KEYS TO SUCCESS

Much more than advertising, marketing views every communication as a chance to enhance your relationship with prospective customers, and it sees current customers as future prospects requiring equal attention.

Strategic marketing is based on an approach of segmenting, targeting, and positioning. This methodology calls for sorting prospective customers according to shared characteristics that impact how they might purchase your product. In the targeting phase, you select attractive segments and customize your approach to them. Positioning consists of tailoring your message to create the desired perception.

The marketing Four Ps—product, price, place, and position—show how each business element participates in communicating to the customer. Product includes specifications, benefits, warranties, and guarantees. Price describes the economics involved, as well as the additional time and energy costs expended in product adoption and use. Place refers to the distribution channel and modes in which your communications and products reach your customers. Finally, position signifies all the elements of your branding and advertising campaign.

These elements only work together if your product provides real value to the customer. In the next chapter, we will discover ways to create a product's revenue stream so the economics accurately reflect the value.

Chapter Quiz

1. STP does *not* include which of the following?
   a. Target
   b. Positioning
   c. Supply
   d. Segmentation
2. Which is *not* part of place?
   a. Segmentation
   b. Distribution
   c. Geography
   d. Specifications
3. Which of the following is *not* necessarily a step in a positioning plan?
   a. Define your goal.
   b. Determine your outsource strategy.
   c. Determine your current position.
   d. Measure and reassess.
4. Marketing activities do *not* include which of the following?
   a. Retaining customers
   b. Forsaking customers
   c. Creating customers
   d. Satisfying customers
5. Which of the following is *not* part of promotion?
   a. Distribution
   b. Advertising
   c. Branding
   d. Publicity
6. Which of the following is *not* a common segmentation scheme?
   a. Demographic
   b. Behavioral
   c. Psychographic
   d. Hagiographic
7. Which of the following is *not* part of product?
   a. Warranties
   b. Segmentation
   c. Specifications
   d. Features

8. Segments must be all of the following except _____ .
   a. accessible
   b. actionable
   c. capable
   d. differentiable
9. Which of the following is *not* part of price?
   a. Segments
   b. Time
   c. Discounts
   d. Energy
10. Which of the following is *not* one of the classic marketing Four Ps?
    a. Promotion
    b. Price
    c. Position
    d. Product

4

VALUE PROPOSITIONS

You buy the holes, not the drill.

—THEODORE LEVITT

I f only one principle summarizes business management theory, it is the value proposition. Unfortunately, because it lies at the intersection of so many disciplines (economics, marketing, and strategy, to name a few), it is often just a signpost on the freeway for a passing business student.

The problem is not limited to business school. Too often product development teams don't tackle the value proposition early enough in the cycle. They only discover it later—when their new product doesn't sell.

DEFINITION OF THE VALUE PROPOSITION

The value proposition motivates your prospect to buy because it demonstrates that the price of your solution is lower than the cost of the problem. Be warned that the marketplace drives price, while management determines the cost of providing the solution. In other words, if you can't control your costs to offer a solution profitably, that is entirely your problem and not that of the marketplace. In Part 2, we will discuss methods to control costs.

CONCEPT

Value Propositions

The *value proposition* motivates your prospect to buy because it demonstrates that the price of your solution is lower than the cost of the problem. It has nothing to do with the cost of production; the marketplace determines the price for a product, while management drives the internal cost to produce it.

In Chapter 3, you learned to segment the market to find your potential customers, target them, and position your product. You also saw how to use the classic Four Ps—product, price, place, and promotion—to reach, satisfy, and retain your customers. We will now discuss building an economic case for purchasing your product.

The cost to buyers may have a number of noneconomic components, such as the time or energy they have dedicated to the problem. The total price includes payment made at the time of purchase and ongoing fees for service contracts, retainer agreements, and other long-term relationships. As Adrian Ott describes in her new book *The 24-Hour Customer*,[1] customers often value time even more highly than the dollars they spend. This insight gives you the opportunity to command a higher price if you save the customer time on a long-term basis.

COMMODITIES AND DIFFERENTIATED PRODUCTS

Before you develop a product, think carefully about creating something that is not a commodity. To avoid this, you need to understand commodities, which are products such as wheat, oil, and rice that are identical, regardless of origin.

CONCEPT

Commodities and Differentiated Products

Commodities are products that are identical, regardless of where they come from. *Differentiated products* have some type of additional value; ideally, your product provides a unique value. As an innovator, you want to develop a differentiated product.

Without anything to differentiate competing products, the marketplace finds an equilibrium price that favors no one manufacturer. Prices, and thus margins, vary with economic conditions. One example is oil; one barrel traded at $147.27 on July 11, 2008, and then at $33.87 on December 21 of the same year. This collapse coincided entirely with the financial crisis and had nothing to do with changes in the oil itself.

You may be saying, "But I have a new gizmo! What does this have to do with oil or rice?" Unfortunately, if you do not provide enough value, your product may find itself priced like rice or oil through the following process, shown graphically in Figure 4-1:

1. A new product appears on the market and commands a high price because it is rare and demand exists.
2. A competing company sees the attractive demand and offers a similar product at a slightly lower price, thus eroding the market share of the original product even as demand increases because of the competition's lower price.

Figure 4-1   Example of Downward Price Pressure

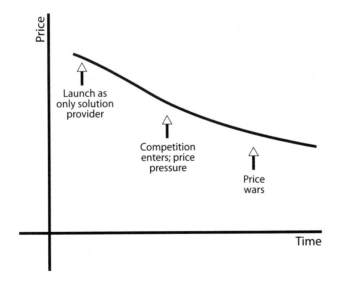

3. The manufacturer of the original product is forced to lower prices. Demand increases as the prices fall yet again in a price war. Even though the volume is growing rapidly, the profit on each product decreases.

Do you think your interesting gizmo is exempt from this life cycle? Consider the cell phone. In 1999, many customers paid $200 for a cell phone, which had exactly one capability: making phone calls. Today, a $200 smartphone can have many more capabilities: text messaging, a digital camera, a video recorder, e-mail, a global positioning system (GPS), WiFi, Bluetooth, ringtone selection, color display, and voice recognition.

If $200 buys you today's smartphone but used to buy you just a cell phone, then the value of an actual cell phone itself is now very low. Cell phones have become commodities. That is, your $200 buys you all the other capabilities—text messaging, camera, and so forth—and the phone itself is cheap.

FEATURES, BENEFITS, AND ECONOMIC VALUE

If you are not offering a commodity, by definition, you must have an added feature. This feature distinguishes your product from a commodity. This does not apply simply to wheat and corn; personal computers have effectively become commodities because they are practically identical in their components and capabilities. Even airline travel (at least in coach) is practically a commodity; how different is a trip on one airline versus another?

A feature is useful only if it adds benefit. The benefit is the improvement that the customer receives from the features. Continuing with the cell phone example, you may be purchasing one and think, "I want GPS service because I need the navigating function, but I already have a great camera and wouldn't use my cell phone this way. Therefore, I'm willing to pay more for a phone with the navigator than a phone with the camera." In this example, the GPS system provided benefits only because you (the buyer) need the navigation system. If you were housebound or had a perfect sense of direction, the navigation system would have no value.

Up to now, it may seem that we have taken an easy process—buying a cell phone—and complicated it. But we need to think about it clearly, because now the customer must quantify the benefit's economic value. The entire thought process is summarized in Figure 4-2.

Figure 4-2   A Product Feature Leads to Benefits with Quantifiable
Economic Value

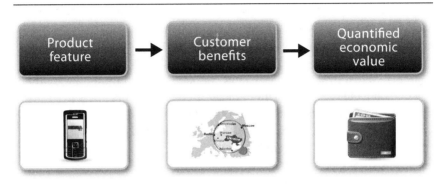

Back to our cell phone example. You might say, "I need navigation, but if the phone costs $1,000, then I'll use my map book instead. If the phone's $50, the navigation is cheap and will save me lots of hassle." The real problem comes in the middle. What happens with a $200 phone? You say, "Gee, that's more than I want to pay for navigation, but maybe I'll use the camera sometimes." Or do you?

For consumer products, it is remarkably difficult to estimate your feature's economic value because people evaluate features according to their own priorities. Some gadget freaks see the $200 phone and say, "Maybe I'd rather pay $150 for the phone with the navigator service, but I'll pay $200 so my friends will think I'm cool." Meanwhile, someone else stops at half the sentence: "I'd rather pay $150 for the phone with the navigator service, so I'll wait." The gadget freak is unlikely to be that honest about his priorities because he may not admit the value he places on being "cool." In fact, this is a current area of research; as economics professor Dan Ariely recently said about the early adopters of a new product, "It's not about the cost-benefit analysis."[2]

This makes business-to-business sales easier in some respects, because prospects with profit-and-loss responsibility can typically articulate the dollar value of the problem or will respond well to a sensible analysis that attempts to value it.

In my experience, engineers especially struggle with this aspect of product development: valuing the customer's benefit is only an approximation.

You will never know the exact quantified economic value. However, you can compare products with different prospective feature sets by considering both the advantage the product provides and the value the customer perceives.

Figure 4-3 illustrates the possible outcomes and associated risks when you offer products with a set of distinct features into a marketplace that places its own value on them. When you offer a product with an advantage that is highly valued by a sufficiently large marketplace (top right), the resulting spike in demand can be difficult to meet. If customers find that your product provides an insufficient solution, they become unhappy (top left). If your advantage is not valued by the marketplace, the demand is too small (bottom right). And if you do not provide an advantage with high value, then your product is simply poorly designed (bottom left).

If you are managing competently, the benefit that you provide exceeds your cost to provide it. This difference is basically your margin. If your product's benefit is significantly differentiated from that of your competitors, and

Figure 4-3   Risks Associated with a Failure to Align the Advantage Provided and the Value Perceived

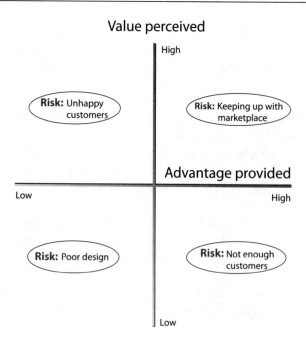

the industry structure has placed significant barriers to entry (see Chapter 2 on strategy) to keep competitors from imitating you, then you are in good shape.

DAMNED IF YOU DON'T

Some value propositions evaluate the cost of *not* having the solution. Products that satisfy government regulations are in this category; for instance, a maker of fire extinguishers benefits from laws requiring store owners to have fire extinguishers. Insurance also falls into this group, since the product's value can easily be compared to the price of not having it. Of course, not all insurance is identical: auto insurance is a "damned-if-you-don't" product because most states require car owners to carry insurance; however, since no such law exists for life insurance, providers must articulate the benefit differently.

Warranties and service agreements also fall into this category. Have you shopped for a printer and been offered a warranty lately? They used to be worthwhile, but now the warranties are often more expensive than the cost of a new printer. The value proposition should include the cost of your time in installing the new printer, but since installation procedures have also become simpler, the case for buying a warranty is not so compelling. It is simply cheaper and easier to replace a printer than to repair it through a warranty.

Damned-if-you-don't value propositions can be effective for lawyers and accountants, because legal and tax reporting problems generate anxiety. However, this sometimes causes resentment toward the provider, so the customer relationship must be handled more carefully. Consultants who can create damned-if-you-don't value propositions often command high fees when the success of the business appears to be at stake.

HINT

Value Propositions for Service Providers

Service providers must clearly articulate their value propositions. Sometimes it is as simple as replacing the cost of an associated employee, such as using an independent lawyer on an hourly basis instead of hiring one to serve as full-time general counsel. For other services, such as those provided by investment bankers, the benefit of the transaction makes the economics easy to calculate. In a sales proposal, a service provider should always evaluate the prospect's return on an investment in the service.

VALUE PROPOSITIONS AND STRATEGIC ELEMENTS

Your product's value proposition must be well tuned to your corporate strategy, or you will trip over yourself in execution. This section describes how your value proposition must align with generic strategies, corporate mission statements, and branding.

Generic Strategies

Chapter 2 summarized how Michael Porter identified the two key strategies for a broad market approach as competing on low price and differentiation. We can look at Wal-Mart and Nordstrom as examples of each of these extremes.

For many years, Wal-Mart used its iconic yellow smiley face as the literal face of the company in advertisements. The cute round face smiled along as prices were visibly lowered in the Rolling Back Prices advertising campaign, and it also appeared on store signage. With its densely packed shelves and labyrinthine layouts, Wal-Mart grew into a colossus. Where else can you buy donuts, car seats, and furniture? Its slogan is "Save money. Live better."

Nordstrom offers a different shopping experience. Products are rarely on sale, a pianist plays in the center of the roomy store, and salespeople speak in calm tones as they slavishly attend to you. Urban legends swirl around the store's customer service, most of them along the lines of "They took back something they don't sell."

Metaphorically speaking, most products lie on a continuum between Wal-Mart and Nordstrom. The manufacturer is competing either on price or on added value. As a product manager, you must determine how your product will compete and which path is aligned with your corporate strategy. Adding features is counterproductive if you are trying to compete strictly on price; you must provide only the minimal feature set required by the buyer. If you want to compete on value, provide features with enough benefits to justify the price.

Corporate Mission Statements

Mission statements (described in Chapter 2) and value propositions should reflect the same philosophy. For instance, Wal-Mart's mission statement is

"To give ordinary folk the chance to buy the same thing as rich people." Therefore, the value proposition at Wal-Mart must reflect lower prices, not added value.

Now consider Disney's mission statement: "To make people happy." This mission does not implicitly state a high cost for alternatives, as the Wal-Mart mission statement does. Indeed, not having the solution—namely, Disney—is equivalent to sadness! As the clever MasterCard advertisements say, "Priceless."

It's not enough to align a product with a mission statement; innovators need to align their product's value proposition with the actual mission, the reason management gets out of bed in the morning. If your company's reason for being is to provide lower costs to buyers, don't load your product with extra features.

Brands

While many books describe branding, my two favorites are the textbook *Marketing Management*, by Philip Kotler and Kevin Lane Keller, and *Positioning: The Battle for Your Mind*, by Al Ries and Jack Trout. This section cannot do justice to this important topic in the available space.

If you want to understand the connection between branding and value propositions, the auto industry is a great place to start. Consider Volvo: its strong safety record is legendary. (Because I was six months pregnant when I bought a Volvo, my husband claimed that it was equivalent to stamping the word *sucker* on my head when I walked into the dealership.) Several years ago, Volvos were the only vehicles available with side air bags, which are now standard from many manufacturers. This breakthrough feature was completely aligned with Volvo's strong brand representing safety.

When you develop your product, it is not enough to align your value proposition with your corporate strategy (broadly speaking, either cost leadership or differentiation). Your features, and thus the value you offer, must be aligned with your brand as well. Some strong consumer brands, such as Louis Vuitton purses and Dom Perignon, convey added value strictly with the brand name; the quality must match the brand.

Choose features that correspond with the image you are trying to project and the position you want to create in the prospect's mind. These notes should all play in harmony.

CONCEPT

The Value Proposition and Strategic Elements

Your value proposition and strategy must be aligned and consistent with your corporate mission. Align your value proposition and brand by adding features consistent with the brand; don't concern yourself with adding too many features if you are trying to compete by offering the lowest price.

PRICING MODELS

Pricing schemes can vary tremendously. We pay for some items before we obtain the benefits (a shirt, a college education); some after receiving the benefits (a restaurant meal, a doctor's visit); and some along the way (a home mortgage, car insurance). This section analyzes different pricing models and how they create value propositions.

The Power Drill

The humble power drill is an example of a straightforward value proposition; as they say, "You buy the holes, not the drill." How does this work?

Suppose you want to hang 40 pictures on the walls of your new house and thus need 40 holes. The cost of borrowing the drill may be lower economically but will take a toll in personal costs, so you need to find a way to make 40 holes.

You look at $20 drills, thinking, "I could use my hammer and a giant nail to make holes. However, that may not work because of the anchors needed for my heavy paintings, so I really need a drill. If I buy the $20 drill and I have to make 40 holes, each hole costs me $0.50. Is each hole worth $0.50? Actually, doing it fast is probably worth even more than that. Plus, once the pictures are hung, I still have the drill—and every hole after that is effectively free."

In this model, the entire price is paid up front, and the company's margin is generated up front as well. After the initial payback, the customer receives ongoing value, but the company does not earn any added revenue.

The Razor Blade Model

We forget today that the first safety razor was a major revolution, because of both its new manufacturing techniques and its novel business model. In the early 1900s, King Camp Gillette exploited the changing manufacturing conditions to structure his sales around a cheap razor and expensive blades, creating the so-called razor blade model. In this structure, you offer an item at a low margin or even at a loss (known as a loss leader) in order to stimulate recurring sales of a more profitable item. The razor is offered at a loss, but the blades generate enough margin to compensate.

Consider a new razor packaged with two razor blades and priced at $13.00. A package of three additional blades is priced at $9.00, so each blade is priced at $3.00; this means the new razor's price must be $7.00.

Now you need assumptions on the blade replacement frequency. Let's assume a buyer changes the blade weekly so that he uses four in a month. The value proposition depends entirely on the number of recurring purchases. For this customer, the value over one month looks like this:

$$\text{Month 1 cost to customer} = 1 \text{ razor} + 4 \text{ blades} = \$7.00 + \$12.00 = \$19.00$$

If having a clean-shaven face for one month is worth more than $19.00, the customer will buy the razor and blades. However, he gets really excited about the calculation in the second month:

$$\text{Month 2 cost to customer} = 4 \text{ blades} = \$12.00$$

The second month's cost of a clean-shaven face is even less than the first month's, as shown in Table 4-1.

Table 4-1   The Razor Blade Model from the Customer's Point of View

Cost to Customer	Month 1	Month 2
Razor	$7.00	$0.00
Blades ($3/blade)	$12.00	$12.00
Total	$19.00	$12.00

Now let's analyze this from the innovator's point of view. Assume you generate a 10 percent profit ($0.70) on each razor and a 50 percent profit ($1.50) on each blade. To your company, the sales look like Table 4-2.

Table 4-2   The Razor Blade Model from the Company's Point of View

| | MONTH 1 | | | MONTH 2 | | |
Item sold	Revenue	Profit	Margin	Revenue	Profit	Margin
Razor	$7.00	$0.70	10%	$0.00	$0.00	10%
Blades	$12.00	$6.00	50%	$12.00	$6.00	50%
Total	$19.00	$6.70	35%	$12.00	$6.00	50%

The win-win situation from the razor blade model is summarized in Table 4-3, showing how everyone wins in Month 2; the customer's cost has decreased, but the company's margin has increased. This is why smart product managers often try to build this structure into their product.

Table 4-3   The Win-Win Nature of the Razor Blade Model

	MONTH 1	MONTH 2
Cost to buyer	$19.00	$12.00
Margin for seller	35%	50%

CONCEPT

Razor Blade Model
In the razor blade model, a *loss leader* motivates the purchase of a more profitable, recurring revenue stream.

Product-Service Packages

Another model with a recurring revenue stream is a product with an ongoing service revenue. Examples include a dishwasher with annual service visits or an accounting firm that charges a fixed fee for a tax return and a monthly retainer for ongoing financial advice.

One fascinating example was described by reporter Saul Hansell in a *New York Times* article.[3] Hansell pointed out that Apple began by offering the iPhone for $399 with $20 per month for Internet access from AT&T, making a total cost of $879 for a two-year contract. However, when the company changed the structure to $199 for the phone plus $30 a month for Internet access, sales increased dramatically, even though the total cost for a two-year contract increased to $919, an increase of $40. These calculations are summarized in Table 4-4.

Table 4-4   Customer Preference Is Not Always Rational

	Plan 1	Plan 2
Phone	$399	$199
Monthly cost	$20	$30
Total cost for two years	$879	$919
Customer preferred	No	Yes

Hansell also describes how the text message prices have doubled in recent years to $0.20 each, even though the associated cost of providing the service is almost zero.

What's happening here? The answer is that cell phone providers have isolated two different aspects of the value proposition. First, the monthly pricing scheme may look familiar to you as another embodiment of the razor blade philosophy, where lower up-front prices motivate the purchase of a recurring revenue stream that is more profitable to the company. For the text messages, however, doubled pricing reflects a better understanding of the value to customers; evidently a text message is worth considerably more than $0.10.

KEYS TO SUCCESS

The value proposition motivates your prospect to buy because it demonstrates that the price of your solution is lower than the cost of the problem. Develop a product with features offering benefits to your prospect, where a benefit is the positive worth that the customer receives from the features. If there is no benefit, then the feature has no value. Your prospect must perceive and quantify economic value in the benefits. Damned-if-you-don't strategies evaluate the cost of not having the solution, even if the problem may not exist (as with insurance and fire extinguishers).

There are intangible elements to value propositions. The value proposition must be aligned with your corporate mission and generic market strategy. It should also be consistent with your corporate brand.

Good examples for understanding value propositions include the power drill, the razor blade, and cell phone contracts. Power drills provide all their value, and thus all the margin to the manufacturer, upon purchase. The razor blade model consists of a loss leader motivating customers to create a more profitable, recurring revenue stream. Cell phone contract structures represent a hybrid of the two.

Warren Buffett once said, "Price is what you pay. Value is what you get." I would adapt this for a manager: "Price is what the market pays, and cost is what I pay." As long as you clearly identify the cost, price, and value, and make sure that they always increase in that order, you will stay in business.

Chapter Quiz

1. **To communicate a value proposition to your customer, which is *not* a step?**
   a. The customer quantifies the benefit's economic value.
   b. The customer cannot quantify the benefit's economic value.
   c. The feature distinguishes your product from a commodity.
   d. The benefit is the improvement the customer receives.
2. **Which statement is *not* true?**
   a. The total price may include service agreements.
   b. The total price may include other long-term relationships.
   c. The total price must be incurred at purchase.
   d. The total price may include retainer agreements.

3. Which field is *not* involved in developing the value proposition?
   a. Strategy
   b. Law
   c. Marketing
   d. Economics

4. Commodities are _____ .
   a. products with unique value
   b. products that are identical, regardless of origin
   c. differentiated products
   d. the innovator's goal

5. A razor blade model consists of _____ .
   a. a revenue stream where the customer loses value in future purchases
   b. an even revenue stream from the first purchase
   c. a loss leader motivating a more profitable, recurring revenue stream
   d. selling the product's entire value in one purchase

6. A value proposition motivates your prospect to buy because it demonstrates that _____ .
   a. the problem has no cost
   b. the cost of the problem is large
   c. the price of the solution is small
   d. the price of your solution is lower than the cost of the problem

7. Which statement is *not* true?
   a. Price wars typically keep prices high.
   b. Prices typically decrease over time.
   c. Prices are typically highest at launch.
   d. Competition typically forces prices down.

8. Your value proposition must align well with all of the following except _____ .
   a. branding
   b. generic strategies
   c. corporate mission statements
   d. vertical integration

9. Damned-if-you-don't products do *not* include _____ .
   a. auto insurance
   b. service agreements
   c. razor blades
   d. warranties

10. **Which statement is *not* true?**
    a. Management determines the solution's price.
    b. The value proposition is concerned with the problem's cost to the buyer.
    c. Management determines the cost of providing the solution.
    d. The marketplace determines the solution's price.

5

INTELLECTUAL PROPERTY

Intellectual property has the shelf life of a banana.
—BILL GATES

R emember high school civics? You may have learned that the U.S. Constitution grants Congress the "Power to promote the Progress of Science and useful Arts, by securing for limited Times to Authors and Inventors the exclusive Right to their respective Writings and Discoveries." Innovators recognize the phrase "exclusive right" as an attractive barrier to entry.

Some businesses have advantages that can't be protected, such as an accountant's ability to be a great listener or a local sandwich shop with a long history in the neighborhood. But these advantages limit the business's growth and keep them small-scale operations.

To create a larger business, you have to scale up systematically and infuse your products with a defensible, proprietary feature that provides real benefits to users. If you have invested time and resources into developing and marketing your product, you should be the only one who benefits. Don't you agree?

DEFINITION OF INTELLECTUAL PROPERTY

In common use, *intellectual property* refers to exclusive rights over the products of creative endeavors. Some intellectual property is registered with the government in exchange for exclusive rights to derive products from it or distribute it; after a fixed term, the innovation passes into the public domain. The government offers you this exclusivity to motivate you to "share the wealth" of your creativity.

Intellectual property registration does not give you the right to a specific action, but you do have the right to exclude or prevent others from taking an action. This means that you don't actually have to use it yourself in order to prevent others from taking advantage of it. Two alternative innovation models circumvent registration systems: maintenance of trade secrets and—its complete opposite—open source innovation.

CONCEPT

Intellectual Property
Intellectual property refers to exclusive rights over the products of creative endeavors.

HINT

Intellectual Property for Service Providers
Service providers often generate tremendous quantities of intellectual property, such as taglines and written works. These can be protected through the copyright process. Service providers then can scale their businesses effectively by selling their copyrighted works through retailers.

CREATING AN EFFECTIVE INTELLECTUAL PROPERTY STRATEGY

As Kevin Rivette and David Kline describe in *Rembrandts in the Attic: Unlocking the Hidden Value of Patents*, intellectual property can play a key role in corporate strategy.[1] Innovators should chart the commercialization and patent paths simultaneously rather than filing for a patent first and hoping for the best. For instance, when Gillette developed its Sensor razor, it was the first to have twin spring-loaded blades. The development team identified and patented seven different designs but ultimately chose to manufacture the design that would be hardest for competitors to circumvent; that is, anyone trying to sell a razor with a similar design would likely infringe on the Gillette patent. The patentable inventions covered predictable items such as the springs and the blade angle; less foreseeable was the set of patents covering the razor's packaging and even high-speed photographic techniques used for close-ups of a person shaving.

Intellectual property and strategy also overlap in the copyright world, where digital distribution has transformed the entire industry. Historically, music publishers took risk by pressing records even when it was unclear if they would sell. The same publishers also managed a distribution network in which every middleman took his own cut off the top. The entire business model rested on recouping the original publication and distribution costs before a single cent of profit could be realized. Book publication worked under the same model.

As digital media began to trump traditional products, the business model changed. Recording artists who were used to selling CDs of nine songs for $12.99 suddenly had to cope with the iTunes Store selling their songs for $0.99 each. As this book goes to press, the book and newspaper industries are in flux.

Today's copyright management includes other marketing elements more than ever. Some say that only established brands such as the *Wall Street Journal* and ESPN will be able to charge for digital content. Certainly these organizations are among the strongest brands in filtered information aggregation; unlike sites like Wikipedia, where the goal is to provide universal access to publication, the established brands prevent "just anyone" from publishing under their marquees. As pricing models evolve in this area, the relationship between copyright management and corporate strategy is sure to change.

BRANDS AND INTELLECTUAL PROPERTY

Intellectual property plays an important role in your marketing strategy because brands can acquire tremendous value. The Interbrand Corporation estimates that in 2009, Coca-Cola was the world's most valuable brand, with an estimated value of $69 billion. This is enough to motivate you to consider branding carefully from the beginning!

The patent portfolio of the Gillette Sensor razor included protection of the packaging. Apparently, the management team wanted the entire experience to reflect the manly, smooth feel associated with the improved shave. When the team integrated this sensibility with the packaging, they patented that as well.

Intel also created extra value for its patent portfolio by stamping computers with the "Intel inside" label. Although computers had contained Intel chips previously, Intel made its patents more valuable by lending its name to confer credibility on products using its chips.

ACCOUNTING CONSIDERATIONS

The entire point of investing in intellectual property protection is not only to recover those costs, but to generate a return. Imagine spending $25,000 to patent an improved buggy whip. Then, after you incur other manufacturing and marketing expenses, you are surprised to find that your buggy whip does not sell. Instead, people are buying hybrid cars.

You may laugh, but companies—especially start-ups—frequently find themselves protecting new buggy whips. If no one will buy the derived product, the intellectual property has no value. You might value the buggy whip patent at $25,000, but it may be worth nothing.

Assigning economic value to intellectual property depends on the specific valuation model, but it should ultimately reflect the sales of derived products. Don't patent a buggy whip.

TYPES OF INTELLECTUAL PROPERTY

This section lists various ways to develop and protect proprietary advantages, skipping over many of the technical details in order to put this activity in context as part of the innovator's toolbox. You can find several good summaries written by real lawyers with up-to-date information, such as *Intellectual Property* by Catherine Holland and others.[2] We'll discuss protecting inventions, creative expressions, and even your business image. The government provides protection for some intellectual property; other elements are protected internally; and other models publicize the "secret sauce" and offer no protection at all.

One note: We will use the U.S. system as the basis for discussion, particularly in connection with the U.S. Patent and Trademark Office (USPTO) and the U.S. Copyright Office. Check with your attorney for guidance on applying for international protection under trade agreements. Note that patents and trademarks are territorial, but copyright protection exists globally without further action.

Patents: Manufacturing Innovation

Patents are issued for manufacturing innovation. The field is dense with technical requirements and a complex filing process, which will not be discussed in depth here because many excellent guides already exist. Work closely with a patent agent or attorney; specialists are certified by the USPTO.

CONCEPT

Patents

A *patent* protects manufacturing innovation. For utility patents (most commonly issued), an innovator must demonstrate that the invention is new, nonobvious, and useful; the other major class is a design patent protecting ornamental elements.

The vast majority of issued patents are classified as "utility," covering the innovation's use. Design patents protect ornamental elements affecting the product's appearance.

Utility patents are issued for processes (developing methods or algorithms), machines (integrating parts and devices), manufacturing (making useful articles from raw materials), and a composition of matter (creating chemical structures and formulations). To patent your innovation, you must demonstrate that it is new, nonobvious, and useful. The USPTO has clear requirements for each of these qualities.

A patent represents a right to exclude, not a right to make or sell your invention; however, if you have improved someone else's protected innovation, you can't sell the improved innovation without that person's/company's permission. The good news is that your patent allows you to stop the original innovator from selling your improvement.

Patents are expensive (filing costs are often around $25,000) to create and maintain, but they provide an avenue for the garage inventor to create something that he or she can shop around or use as the basis for a company. They can also be an enormous drain on time and money if you don't have a good understanding of the marketplace. Thousands of issued patents have absolutely no value because they represent the output of an extended tinkering effort, not a viable product.

Utility patents are valid for 20 years from the date of filing (barring some rare exceptions), while design patents are valid for 14 years. This may seem like a long time, but if you consider that the patent is the first piece in the puzzle before any manufacturing effort or sales campaigns take place, 20 years can actually go very quickly. The pharmaceutical industry is populated by executives terrified of the patent expiration dates of their blockbuster drugs. Although it may seem that these companies extend their patents, once the original patent expires, the old molecule is then usually manufactured as a "generic" drug. Pharmaceutical companies then often introduce a minor improvement in the molecule so that they can initiate a new patent.

Patent protection is absolutely crucial for many new products, but it is far from a guarantee of success. It protects and defends your market position, but it doesn't create it!

MINICASE

Mach 3 Requires 35 Patents

As described in Rivette and Kline's *Rembrandts in the Attic*, Gillette's Mach 3 razor was introduced in 1998. The company's new proprietary "diamond-like coating" produced blades 10 times thinner and harder than their predecessors; the blade design, revolutionary at the time, consisted of three staggered blades and a forward pivot point. Nearly 200 pieces of equipment and technology resulted from $750 million in development costs; ultimately, the company protected its new technology with 35 patents.[3]

Copyrights: Creative Expression

Copyrights are a set of exclusive rights granted by a government to copy, distribute, or adapt a creative work. Copyrights cover literary and musical works, as well as graphic, audiovisual, and architectural designs. This protection typically lasts for the life of the author plus 70 years, although there are some exceptions.

Copyrights protect the expression of an idea but not the idea itself. Ideas are free; eloquence is proprietary.

CONCEPT

Copyrights
Copyrights are a set of exclusive rights granted by a government to copy, distribute, or adapt a creative work.

For entrepreneurs developing new manufactured goods, copyright protection is less critical than patents, although it is important in protecting website content and design. However, for service providers seeking to expand their businesses, copyright protection is key; many lawyers, accountants, and financial service providers write and self-publish information about their area of expertise to create credibility.

An employee's work created within the scope of employment automatically belongs to the employer and, in fact, the employer is considered the author. Similarly, contractors may generate creative work for others under "work for hire" or "work made for hire" agreements that assign copy and distribution rights back to the client. Employers should be careful to obtain copyright assignment agreements from anyone who is not an employee, such as consultants, advertising agents, photographers, and programmers.

Website content is covered by copyright law; all innovators and businesses should refrain from publishing others' information on their sites without permission, including any reprints. When building your website, always link to related pages rather than usurping material with the cut-and-paste function; obtain permission when necessary.

Authors retain the right to create, copy, or distribute their own work. Good practice calls for use of the copyright symbol ©, the author's name, and the year of first publication; this is not necessary to maintain protection, but it does deter innocent infringement in which someone claims not to realize that he is infringing. Registration is not required to preserve protection, but it is needed to sue for infringement; you must register with the U.S. Copyright

Office within three months of publication. Registration before infringement entitles the registrant to attorney's fees in most cases; this can be a potent weapon in battling infringement.

Trademarks: Brands

A *trademark* is a distinctive word, phrase, symbol, or design, or combination of these used by a business to identify itself as the point of origin of its product, while a service mark identifies the point of origin of a service.[4] Intellectual property specialist Jeff Sheldon explains that "Kodak" is a trademark for cameras, which are goods, but it is also a service mark for a service to process digital pictures. Trademarks are often the brand name of the product and may include graphic elements.

Many innovators enjoy the process of naming a product or company. To do so, you should be aware of how trademark protection increases with the creativity of the mark. Marks fall into four general categories of protection:

- **Descriptive mark:** Just like its name indicates, this mark describes the product. To be protected, you have to invest heavily in marketing so that the word acquires secondary meaning or so that you can show evidence that customers recognize the word as distinctive to your company. An example is Windows software.
- **Suggestive mark:** A mark that suggests something about the product without being too descriptive. An example is HeatShift, a technology used to cool consumer electronics by dissipating the heat.
- **Arbitrary mark:** Uses a real word for a purpose unrelated to the use of the mark. An example is a Coach purse; coaches and purses are not related.
- **Fanciful mark:** An invented word that becomes identified with a product, such as Kleenex.

In order to have protection and prosecute infringement cases, you must show that you are defending your mark. For products, it is appropriate to use the trademark symbol (™) for unregistered marks and the registration symbol (®) for marks registered through the USPTO. Registration is optional but strongly recommended.

One dilemma for innovators is that when a mark is used frequently in print without being prosecuted vigorously it becomes "genericized" and thus loses protection. For this reason, Google has an extensive campaign telling people to refer to their technology as the "Google search engine"; actively enforcing the use of "search engine" in conjunction with the company's name maintains its protection. For a marketer, however, such generic use signifies positioning success. Do you ask for a Kleenex or a tissue?

MINICASE

Swoosh!

In 1971, Nike founder Phil Knight paid a graphic designer, Carolyn Davidson, $35 to design the swooping checkmark. The return on this investment was impressive when you consider that in 2009, Interbrand ranked Nike the 26th most valuable brand in the world, worth $13.1 billion. (Years after the mark was first used, Knight supposedly gave Davidson a diamond ring engraved with the swoosh and an envelope with an undisclosed amount of Nike stock.)

Trade Secrets

Unlike intellectual property registered with the government, trade secrets retain their protection until the secret is disclosed; a well-known example is the formula for Coca-Cola, which has been a trade secret since 1919. Today, urban legends surrounding this mystery include one in which each of the corporation's top two executives have half the formula; another claims that two people have the formula at any given time and are not allowed to fly on the same airplane. Which is it? I don't know. Certainly it is true that no matter how many people actually have access to the entire formula, it remains one of the world's best-kept secrets.

CONCEPT

Trade Secrets

Trade secrets retain their protection until the secret is disclosed.

Trade secrets have the advantage of costing only as much as it takes to keep the secret and are protected indefinitely. Unlike patents and copyrights, trade secrets include proprietary information such as customer lists, internal training programs and workshops, and other organizational know-how.

The lack of registration makes trade secrets harder to defend. Furthermore, while patents are likely to come under attack from outside sources, the weakest link for a trade secret is a disgruntled former employee. Therefore, the best protection for trade secrets involves good personnel procedures, such as controlled use of company logbooks and records and strong nondisclosure agreements.

In general, trade secrets are hard to enforce but do work. Do you have the recipe for Coca-Cola?

MINICASE

Protecting the Colonel's Secret Spice Recipe

On February 10, 2009, Kentucky Fried Chicken issued a press release stating that armed guards had accompanied Colonel Sanders's handwritten "original recipe" to the company's new headquarters.

Open Source Models

Although intellectual property discussions typically sidestep open source innovation because it is not protected, many innovators have considered developing their core components this way, so we will touch on it here. Open source innovation is a process that promotes free access to and free use of core technology without copyright or patent restrictions. This modern movement began in the 1980s when Richard Stallman, a computer scientist at MIT, initiated a project to develop a free computer operating system. Since then, the model has extended beyond software development into pharmaceuticals and other endeavors where specialists self-organize to develop an innovation for the greater good.

CONCEPT

Open Source Innovation
Open source innovation is a process that promotes free access to and free use of core technology without copyright or patent restrictions.

Open source innovation is typically defined by a few key characteristics:

- **Licensing framework:** The use of work created under open source models is typically governed by free licenses or by "copyleft" protection (to differentiate it from *copyright*), which allows for free distribution, even if changes are made to the work.
- **Relentless improvement:** Because of the movement's semirebellious history, open source innovation tends to have a decidedly hackerlike feel. The tone of communication is skeptical, organization is loose, and peer review is frequent. These products tend to evolve constantly in a continuous state of self-directed improvement and a product is declared "ready" when a consensus emerges.
- **Strong accountability:** Much of the original open source software was developed by skilled programmers moonlighting after hours. Loose coordination of thousands of volunteer programmers led to strong individual accountability as code was improved.

Open source product development is effective but problematic when it is linked to free products. The value proposition architecture discussed in Chapter 4 depends on the customer paying for the benefits.

Fortunately, "open source" describes both an economic model and a cultural outlook. You can keep some of the spirit of open source development without sacrificing the financial benefits. Many of the organizational management tools discussed in Chapters 7 and 8 honor the spirit of open source culture by promoting innovation from all levels of the organization, measuring progress transparently, and demanding accountability.

MONETIZING INTELLECTUAL PROPERTY

Other than a few idealists looking to make the world a better place, most innovators believe that the entire point of developing and protecting intellectual property is to monetize it—that is, to generate new revenues from products derived from the protected property. This section summarizes the three principal models for commercializing intellectual property; they can be used independently or in combination. Even though the deal terms may vary, they boil down to the same three options.

Product Creation

In this model, you figure out how to do it, then you do it. Part 2 of this book concerns itself with the creation process, including design, engineering, distribution, and launch.

If you are a garage inventor with a patent, you will find that this process is expensive and ambitious; after we have covered distribution and quality control, it may look more attractive to have someone else do it. The execution challenges are formidable indeed, and the expense and long time frame may make it difficult to raise money from investors or bankers (covered in the next chapter). However, it always exists as an option.

Assignment

An assignment is the permanent and irrevocable transfer of patent ownership. This is equivalent to an unconditional sale of the intellectual property. Payment terms may be a single, lump-sum payment or an extended schedule.

Often this process takes place when an inventor is issued a patent and then founds a company, transferring the intellectual property rights to the company so it can raise investment funds.

CONCEPT

Assignment
An *assignment* is the permanent and irrevocable transfer of patent ownership. This is equivalent to an unconditional sale of the intellectual property.

Assignment may also be attractive to mitigate commercialization risk by a licensee. If you are an inventor and are concerned that your innovation is interesting but difficult to monetize, you may consider assignment so you can wash your hands of the entire matter and cash out.

The trade-off lies between the risk that you (the potential licensee) will be unable to commercialize the intellectual property yourself and your desire to participate in long-term success. Other risk factors may include a changing regulatory environment, an economic shift affecting supply or demand, or market changes that mean the core technology is no longer favored.

Innovators trying to incorporate new technology in their products can often negotiate a patent sale and assignment from a solo inventor. Universities and research institutions typically prefer license agreements to outright sales and assignments. They optimize the success of a start-up company by taking equity in the company and allowing it to defer repayment of the patent expenses until sales exceed a prescribed threshold. This is an ideal arrangement because it aligns the interests of everyone involved: the inventors, the research organization, the management team, and the investors.

Licenses

A license agreement is used more frequently than assignment because its terms allow either party to revoke the agreement. In exchange for the right to exploit the intellectual property, the licensee pays a royalty stream over the unexpired life of the patent.

CONCEPT

License

A *license agreement* confers on an entity other than the patent holder the rights to exploit the intellectual property. The terms and conditions can be structured such that the agreement can be altered or revoked.

MINICASE

City of Hope and Genentech

In the 1970s, before modern licensing strategies had been developed, the research institution City of Hope National Medical Center gave key patents to Genentech, Inc., a fledgling biotechnology company, in exchange for a 2 percent royalty stream. More than 20 years later, City of Hope sued Genentech for violating the royalty agreement, claiming breach of contract rather than patent infringement.

Genentech had already paid City of Hope $300 million in royalties over the years, but it had licensed the technology to other parties. City of Hope successfully claimed that it was owed royalties on another 35 license agreements with other companies based on the original patents and was awarded $300 million in 2002. This successful suit speaks to the importance of diligently executing intellectual property licensing terms—but also to the lengthy time frames associated with recognizing the fruits of those labors.

Defending Your Inventions

When it comes to intellectual property, an ounce of prevention really is worth a pound of cure. Median values for awarded damages in patent cases can be as high as $30 million for lawsuits in the telecommunications industry, although in most other businesses the average is around $8 million.[5] Patent holders are typically successful about one-third of the time. What can you do to protect your inventions and trade secrets? Jeff Sheldon offers some tips:[6]

- **Be discreet.** Assume that any disclosure to customers, consultants, and vendors will not remain confidential, even with signed confidentiality agreements.

- **Develop intellectual property privately.** Discussing ideas in front of customers or consultants can lead to claims of co-ownership, so listen to their feedback and then solve problems in their absence.
- **Negotiate carefully.** Monitor contract terms such as invention assignment, confidentiality clauses, and related provisions that limit your ability to compete with your invention.
- **Document your improvements.** Keep current log books and other notes to show the development of your invention.

Defending Your Brand

Like patents, trademarks and brand names are also subject to infringement. Counterfeiting is a particularly serious concern for manufacturers of branded consumer goods; the United States Immigration and Customs Enforcement (ICE) seized $200 million in counterfeit goods in 2009 alone.[7] Ross Epstein, head of the Intellectual Property Enforcement Practice at The Nath Law Group, recommends several simple and relatively inexpensive ways to defend your product from counterfeiting.[8]

- **Register your trademarks with U.S. Customs.** Record your trademarks with U.S. ICE so that they can actively monitor imports.
- **Create repositories of your IP around the world.** Designate local law firms as repositories of up-to-date information on your intellectual property in other countries.
- **Demonstrate that you are serious.** Although it is difficult to stop every illegal factory making your product (or legal ones making your product during off-hours operations), select a significant manufacturer to make your statement by initiating legal action; you can partner with local law firms, particularly for Asian infringement.
- **Monitor Internet activity.** Keep a close eye on Internet distributors and submit takedown requests wherever you find counterfeit products advertised.

KEYS TO SUCCESS

The sophisticated field of intellectual property management is often the key to a new product. You create something original and want to defend your effort; our intellectual property protection system ensures that you retain the sole right to commercialize your developments.

Patents and copyrights protect inventions and creative expression, respectively. Patents protect innovations in core technology and offshoots such as novel tooling, packaging methods, and other processes. Any invention protected in this way must be novel, nonobvious, and useful. Creative expressions such as websites, marketing copy, and other written materials are protected by copyright even if they are not registered; however, registration is required to prosecute infringement.

Trademarks include slogans, logos, and other methods that identify a specific company—whether service provider or manufacturer—as the point of origin for its products. Not all trademarks are created equal; more creative and inventive names represent stronger marks than descriptive or suggestive marks.

The two extremes for product development outside the realm of protected intellectual property are trade secrets and open source innovation. Unlike innovations protected by the U.S. government, trade secrets are protected for the life of the kept secret. On the other hand, open source innovation is developed publicly and distributed under free license models.

To commercialize intellectual property, you must derive a product from it, assign it, or license it. Creating a product requires design, manufacturing, and distribution; these functions may be performed internally or outsourced. Assignment is a permanent and irrevocable change of ownership, whereas license agreements are revocable or alterable under clearly defined terms. Assignment typically shifts the risk from the inventor to the assignee and takes place in conjunction with a patent sale, paid as a lump sum or on a staggered schedule. License agreements allow the inventor to retain some rights if the terms of the agreement are violated; they are commonly used in university start-ups and other organizations willing to retain some risk in exchange for long-term interest in the technology.

Intellectual property management interacts strongly with strategy, marketing, and accounting. Strategic considerations for patents include deriving products from patents whose designs are difficult to circumvent. The strategy also depends on contemporary distribution and marketing models; digital distribution methods have transformed copyright management strategies. Marketing considerations include protection of strong brands and associated innovations such as packaging methods. Accounting issues revolve around the valuation of intellectual property; the property is typically valued at the cost of protecting it until it is monetized.

Think about the commercialization path and the eventual outcome before you spend a fortune protecting intellectual property. You may take a different path than you might have anticipated.

Chapter Quiz

1. Which of the following statements is *not* true?
   a. A license agreement is irrevocable.
   b. A license agreement can be revoked.
   c. A license agreement confers the rights to exploit intellectual property.
   d. A license agreement is written with terms and conditions.
2. Why do service providers have difficulty raising investment money for their intellectual property?
   a. Service providers have nothing to protect.
   b. There is no way to scale a service provider's intellectual property.
   c. Commercialization usually requires the originator.
   d. Service providers do not generate much intellectual property.
3. Which is *not* a type of trademark?
   a. Fanciful mark
   b. Suggestive mark
   c. Arbitrary mark
   d. Creative mark
4. Accounting considerations for intellectual property do *not* include which of the following?
   a. The idea that the intellectual property does not lead to eventual sales
   b. Expected sales of the product derived from the intellectual property
   c. The goal of expecting a return on the investment
   d. The use of different valuation models
5. Patents are issued for _____.
   a. marks of identification
   b. manufacturing innovation
   c. creative expression
   d. novel revenue models

6. Which of the following statements is *not* true?
   a. Copyrights are exclusive rights.
   b. Copyrights cover creative works.
   c. Copyrights protect ideas.
   d. Copyrights protect expression.

7. Which of the following statements is *not* true?
   a. All trademarks have the same level of protection.
   b. You should use different symbols for unregistered and registered marks.
   c. Genericized trademarks are a sign of positioning failure.
   d. You must show that you are defending your mark to prosecute infringement.

8. Open source innovation does *not* necessarily include which characteristic?
   a. Strong accountability
   b. A novel licensing framework
   c. Relentless improvement
   d. Maximized profitability

9. Which of the following is *not* a way of commercializing intellectual property?
   a. Assigning it
   b. Leaving it alone
   c. Deriving a product from it
   d. Licensing it

10. *Intellectual property* refers to _____ .
    a. cost-effective product development
    b. guaranteed revenue streams
    c. exclusive rights over the products of creative endeavors
    d. new products

6

FUNDING

An entrepreneur without funding is a musician
without an instrument.

—ROBERT A. RICE JR.

Where's my *!#* check? You may have asked this before, but now you can channel your inner Jerry Maguire and tell people, "Show me the money!" After all, by now you've learned about many key issues that drive the planning of a new product. Your new product concept is well aligned with your corporate strategy. You're ready to market from the outset, you can articulate the economic benefits with an effective value proposition, and you're prepared to protect the results of all this creative energy with an intellectual property plan.

Now you are ready to spend some money! You need a good marketing person on staff and perhaps a patent attorney. You are also getting down to the nuts and bolts of equipment and inventory needs. Who will write the check? How does that person make a decision?

This chapter is an introduction to the lingo of capital allocation. Once you understand the vocabulary, you'll be able to think like the guy with the checkbook. We will discuss the basic elements determining the worth of your product; although the mechanics are different for product managers and start-up companies, the concepts are the same.

The mathematics needed to actually conduct these calculations are beyond the scale of this book. However, after reading this material, you should have a better handle on the decision-making process behind the check. Consult an accountant or a finance professional for specific guidance on product valuation.

VALUATION AND FINANCE

Like it sounds, valuation is the estimate of the total value of your product. Product managers and entrepreneurs face different challenges in this area. If you're a product manager who is expanding existing product lines, you probably have a good handle on forecasting expected revenues and can decently estimate market shares, market penetration rates, and other parameters. Your organization may also have manufacturing facilities that can accommodate another product in test phases and operations. Finally, if you don't have good data, you can probably access the corporate marketing department with a (limited) budget for subject matter experts.

By definition, entrepreneurs strike out into uncharted territory. They typically do not have good market data and cannot afford expensive reports. Furthermore, they are often inexperienced in the specifics of getting a product off the ground and do not estimate capital requirements well.

For this reason, each group uses a different methodology to value a new product. Product managers use a discounted cash flow analysis to value their product, while entrepreneurs use other less rigorous metrics. Let's go through the ideas behind each one so you can find ways to successfully fund your project.

CONCEPT

Valuation

Valuation is the estimate of the total value of your product. It is used as the basis for investment decisions.

RISK

You probably have thought about risk if you've dabbled in the stock market. Stocks or bonds? Blue-chip companies in the United States or smaller companies in Latin America? When you make these decisions, you are estimating risk and expected return.

Investment decisions are guided by risk assessments, where we will define risk as the probability of an unfavorable outcome. As you learned in Chapter 1, product development entails three general categories of risk: supply risk, demand risk, and execution risk. When you propose your new product to a funding source, the person holding the checkbook is evaluating risk.

No risk assessment protocol is perfect—as anyone who lived through a financial crisis can attest. For this reason, if you want to fund your project, you should honestly assess the risks associated with its success.

One key principle of operating as a free market is that we expect to be compensated more for taking bigger risks. Therefore, if your product appears to have a high risk, your funding source will expect a higher return in exchange.

CONCEPT

Risk

Risk is the probability of an unfavorable outcome. It is a key parameter in investment decisions. In a free market, we expect higher returns for investments with higher risk.

TIME VALUE OF MONEY

The other key driver behind investment decisions is called the time value of money. This is a fancy way of saying that a dollar today is worth more than a dollar tomorrow. People use this expression but not the converse; namely, that tomorrow's dollar is worth less today, and next week's dollar is worth way less than that.

The time value of money is a mathematical formulation that describes money growing or shrinking over time. It may grow at an interest rate, as in a bank, or decline at a discount rate if you tie up funds.

This means that an important part of your valuation is the time it takes for your product to reach the market. If your product requires eight years to develop, it is going to be less competitive than one that takes three years. However, if your product generates significantly higher returns, it may be worth the wait.

CONCEPT

Time Value of Money

The *time value of money* describes how the value of money decreases over the course of time, putting mathematics behind "a dollar today is better than a dollar tomorrow."

FINANCE FOR PRODUCT MANAGERS

Product managers live with less risk than entrepreneurs. In general, when Procter & Gamble considers introducing a whitening toothpaste, the company already has a good sense of the time needed to develop the new formulation, the marketing expenses, and how many people will switch from "minty" to "whitening" toothpaste.

Of course, missteps do happen. One product launch that inadvertently became the gold standard for product failures was Coca-Cola's introduction of New Coke in 1985. The company spent two years developing the new formula, and it succeeded in focus groups. However, people ultimately wanted Coke to taste like Coke, and the product failed.

The good news if you are a product manager in a large organization is that the company will probably survive your glitch. Even Coca-Cola is still standing and is, in fact, quite strong after the failure of New Coke. For that reason, your product is considered independently of the rest of the company (unlike an entrepreneur's product).

Large organizations that expand existing product lines typically understand their markets well and can generate reasonably accurate forecasts using the analytical tools introduced in this chapter. The mathematics are complicated, but the concepts are straightforward. Cash in is better than cash out. Sooner is better than later.

Competition for Product Managers Looking for Funding
Your competition is not just other companies selling similar products, but other products in development at your own company. For instance, pharmaceutical companies constantly evaluate drug candidate efficacy and anticipated marketing needs to determine where to place bets. Take note of the other products under development in your organization.

Discounted Cash Flow Analysis

"Cash is king." Have you ever started a new job in a new city? You have to rent an apartment, buy clothes, buy food—and then you start your job and get paid. Cash goes out before it comes in.

You may have impressive forecasts of your product's $100 million market, but you need to convert those into cash flow projections. You can already imagine how frightening it looks. In the initial phases, you invest in research and development, buying capital equipment, marketing, and building inventory—all requiring that cash go out the door. Later, cash comes in when you generate sales and are no longer spending on development. This process is summarized in Figure 6-1.

Discounted cash flow analysis is a mathematical tool to account for the time value of money and weighted toward faster cash flows. Once you have calculated the cash flows, you discount them back to the present day to figure out the total value of your product.

What does "discounting them back" mean? A discounted cash flow is roughly analogous to putting money in the bank. Imagine getting 5 percent annual interest on your deposit. So if you deposit $1.00, you will get back $1.05 in a year.

Discounting back reverses the problem to start with next year's withdrawal. So if you plan to withdraw $1.05 next year, you discount it back at 5 percent to get $1.00. Next year's $1.05 is worth today's $1.00. The declining value of a dollar is shown graphically in Figure 6-2.

What's the rate that you use as a product manager? The company will likely have its own discount rate that includes risk factors, opportunity cost

Figure 6-1   Cash Flows for a Product Development Project

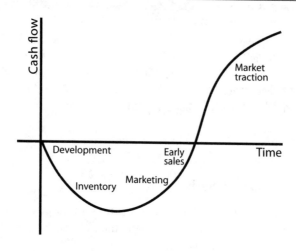

Figure 6-2   The Declining Value of a Dollar in the Future

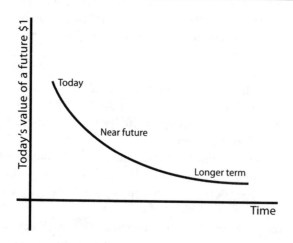

(these dollars can't be invested elsewhere if they are invested with you), cost of capital (the company itself may borrow money to fund your project), and other factors. You can see how different discount rates compare in Figure 6-3. Steeper curves reflect higher discount rates, which translate to higher risk.

Figure 6-3   Comparison of Discount Rates and Risk

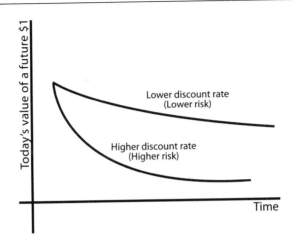

If you're not mathematically inclined, just keep in mind that sooner is better than later for generating cash.

CONCEPT

Discounted Cash Flow

Discounted cash flow analysis is a mathematical tool to account for the time value of money and weighted toward faster cash flows.

Net Present Value

If you discount back all your future cash flows and add them together, you will come up with a single number: the net present value (NPV), or the value of your product today. This number gives you a good estimate of your product's worth. By comparing the NPV of multiple opportunities, the check writer can evaluate which product is worth the investment. This is shown graphically in Figure 6-4.

If the NPV is zero, then all the cash out exactly balances the investment you made. If it is negative, then you lose money on it; the cash out exceeds

Figure 6-4   Building the Net Present Value from Cash Flows

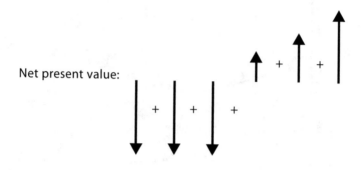

the cash in. The NPV must be positive for the product to be a worthwhile investment. In other words, the cash out has to exceed the cash in, just as your salary has to exceed your rent and other expenses.

CONCEPT

Net Present Value

The *net present value (NPV)* is the sum of the discounted cash flows for your product and gives the value of that product today. The NPV must be positive for the investment to make money.

Internal Rate of Return

As you read a moment ago, the NPV tells you the value of your product today, assuming a discount rate. The internal rate of return (IRR) turns the problem around and asks, at what discount rate does the NPV equal zero? In other words, what's the return rate that makes the cash in exactly balance the cash out? That is the IRR. Internal rates of return are higher for more attractive projects.

The IRR is an important metric used to compare different projects and determine capital allocation strategies. It is known as "internal" because it does not include external risks like inflation or risks associated with your forecasting assumptions. It is used strictly to prepare capital budgets. Imagine comparing projects with two vastly different profiles this way: one project has a long, slow development cycle; the other is more expensive in the short term but ramps up to more significant sales. By calculating their IRRs and seeing which is higher, you can create an apples-to-apples comparison, such as the schematic in Figure 6-5.

Finance teams typically have a minimum, or hurdle, rate of return; your IRR has to exceed this minimum. The best way to generate a higher IRR is to generate cash faster. Long product development cycles lead to poor IRRs, as do products that require a lot of cash going out without high sales volumes to compensate.

CONCEPT

Internal Rate of Return
The *internal rate of return (IRR)* is the discount rate at which the NPV equals zero. It is used internally within an organization to compare projects for capital budgeting purposes.

Figure 6-5 Comparison of the Internal Rates of Return for Two Projects with Different Cash Flow Projections

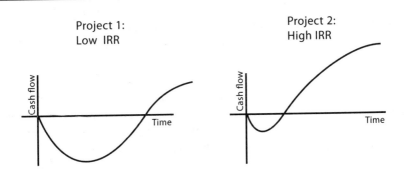

Payback Period

The payback period is exactly what it sounds like: the time needed for the investment to pay for itself. If you spend $100,000 marketing your product and generate $50,000 in sales the first year and $50,000 the second year, the marketing investment has a two-year payback period.

Unlike the other concepts already discussed, the payback period does not include the time value of money (a dollar today is worth more than a dollar tomorrow) or any risks. Instead, it gives you a "quick and dirty" view into your product's financial performance.

CONCEPT

Payback Period

The *payback period* refers to the time needed for an investment to pay for itself. It does not include effects of the time value of money.

FINANCE FOR ENTREPRENEURS

Entrepreneurs finance more than product development; they finance the entire company! In general, they can fund product development through three principal sources: friends and family, private investors, and public investors. The good news is that you don't need to select just one or even just two of these sources. Some successful start-ups leverage all three.

Entrepreneurs with novel products can find private and public resources. Discounting family and friends, the first outside investors in your company are typically angels, individuals who invest their own funds in your company. As you grow, you may reach out to venture capital firms, professionally managed companies with a significantly larger asset base and other resources.

Public funds support the creation of local jobs and focus on generating innovation. Because most are given as grants or loans, the government does not hold any of your stock, which makes investors happy. On the other hand, these loans must be secured, usually by your personal assets.

Leverage both these channels to build a sizable war chest. Seek information on all these sources, and your company will grow to be a robust, formidable force.

HINT

Competition for Entrepreneurs Looking for Funding
Your competition is not just the other manufacturers of your product, but the other deals at the table. In other words, *every* potential investment at the time that you seek funding is effectively your competition. This applies to private investors and public funding alike. Your deal must provide compelling investment terms and other benefits to compete successfully. Use marketing principles (the Four Ps and a focus on creating, satisfying, and retaining customers) early in the process to attract funding.

Friends, Family, and Fools

Did your mom ever lend you the lawnmower so you could cut the neighbors' grass and earn spending money? Businesses large and small have been funded this way. The first round of funding is often called friends and family money (jaded folks just call it "friends, family, and fools," or FFF, money.)

The process of starting a company is beyond the scope of this book, as it obviously requires significant thought and research. Before you deposit a single check from Mom, be sure to talk with your accountant and lawyer about developing a structure that works for your business.

Angel Investors and Venture Capitalists

Many entrepreneurs find it glamorous to start a funding round, in which they reach out to investors. They pepper their conversation with "I talked to a VC," and "We've got some angels looking at us."

The reality can be less glamorous—an infinite string of meetings, people analyzing every aspect of your business plan, others criticizing the product you have carefully conceived. How do you deal with this?

Investors say no far more often than they say yes. (Don't you do the same when you go shopping?) Investment in your deal is not an entitlement or a right, but an opportunity—for both of you. Let's discuss the key elements of the thought process behind private investment.

Angel Investors

Angels are typically savvy professionals who invest their own funds. They buy in under a more formal process than getting a check from your mom, asking for certain investors' rights, such as a seat on your board of directors and the right to cash out first in an exit (sale of the company). All these issues are captured in a "term sheet" summarizing the key investment issues under discussion prior to investment.

Angels may buy debt—that is, they are providing you with a loan—or equity, meaning they buy stock. Whichever investment they make, they expect to get their money back and are thus keenly interested in what is called the "exit strategy." They are thinking about a way out even as they are on the way in! When will you start repaying the loan? When can they exchange their stock for cash or a publicly traded stock? Either of these is a possibility if another company acquires yours.

You can find angel groups easily because they want to find good deals. At first, search the Internet or attend events geared toward entrepreneurs. However, you will have more luck using your personal network, such as your lawyer or accountant, and asking for introductions. These warm connections often pave the way to a straightforward investment process.

To raise angel money successfully, think like a "young big company" rather than a "small business." Show how you will grow and present a plan to scale your business. Do not sigh in relief that this investment will enable you to go on a vacation for the first time in years.

The bottom line is that angels look for and invest in good people. The more trustworthy you are, the easier it is to find money.

Venture Capitalists

Venture capital (VC) firms, cynically known as "vulture capital firms," represent the next step on the ladder. Unlike angels, VC firms invest other people's money, typically those of corporate investors or public pension plans.

Venture capital firms take large risks and thus expect significant returns. Partners in these firms tend to believe strongly in the importance of experienced management and will bring in people who have run similar operations in larger companies to both review the operation during the due diligence process and possibly manage it after the investment takes place.

Like angels, venture capital firms use term sheets and expect special rights. Even though your company will be more mature by the time it reaches this level, there is still significant risk associated with the investment; specifically that the product, and thus the company, may fail before its stock is easily traded. This is why you need to demonstrate that you are thinking about the way out before VC firms get in.

HINT

Value Propositions for Start-Up Deals

If you are in the process of raising money for your start-up company, you must communicate two value propositions to your investors: (1) convince customers to buy your product, and (2) motivate investors to buy into your company.

Public Sources of Funds

Through the Small Business Administration (SBA), the U.S. government offers programs to help finance growth in small businesses. Entrepreneurs who don't want to sell stock or ownership in their companies prefer these vehicles. The catch is that such loans are usually personally guaranteed.

The SBA loans are administered through several different programs. The 7(a) loan program is delivered through commercial lending institutions and provides loans for broad uses. The SBA also runs a microloan program (for loans of less than $50,000) to finance inventory, supplies, and smaller machines and equipment.

The SBA's research grants are more useful to entrepreneurs who develop technical products. The Small Business Innovation Research program is particularly popular and creates interesting opportunities for good technologies. A related program is the Small Business Technology Transfer program that establishes partnerships between small businesses and universities or research institutions.

Government research grants can provide excellent sources of funding for technology product development, because the company does not have to give up stock or repay a loan. This looks good, but beware! On occasion, a government grant can turn into a Bataan death march if the grant's requirements are not in line with the path to commercialization. Meeting the grant milestones can send innocent companies spiraling into dissolution or bankruptcy.

Some products qualify for tax incentives and loan programs at the county or state level for areas of interest to the government. For instance, inventors developing "green" products may find additional funding opportunities to bring their products to maturity and thus to market.

HINT

Funding for Service Providers

If you are a service provider, you are fortunate in that you do not need to invest very much to develop a new product; your only resource is precious time. Thus, unlike product managers and entrepreneurs, you face a different type of competition for funding your product development: your current projects. You have to decide how to allocate time to your ongoing projects and new product development. The good news is that you are the one making the decision, but that also means that you have to look at your business dispassionately, like any investor would. If you find that you are short on cash, it may be possible for you to obtain credit if you have been in business for a while.

KEYS TO SUCCESS

The good news is that you have grown your product concept to a point where you can no longer manage the entire project yourself. Broadly speaking, anyone considering writing a check for your product development is worried about the risk of the product's failure and the time value of money—namely, that a dollar today is worth more than a dollar tomorrow. Investors expect to be compensated well for taking greater risks or waiting longer for success.

Product managers in large organizations must generate forecasts that demonstrate that a product has a positive net present value—that is, that the product will make more than it costs. They may also have to demonstrate that the revenue stream has a high internal rate of return. Finally, the payback time should be reasonable.

Entrepreneurs can look to their friends for initial funding, turning next to both private investors and public sources of funds. Private investors look for governance rights and privileges, regardless of whether they are lending money or buying company stock. Public funds are typically loans backed by personal guarantees, but sometimes they are provided in the form of grants, tax incentives, or other programs.

Service providers typically cannot look to external funding sources, although lines of credit are occasionally available for established businesses. Mostly, they must cannibalize time from their existing projects to create new products.

This can be a stressful process, but it is also very exciting! One way or another, you will have a check in your hand. Now the real work begins.

Chapter Quiz

1. Service providers typically _____ .
   a. have no competition in allocating resources
   b. invest in their new products with time
   c. cannot look at their businesses like investors
   d. have no access to credit financing
2. Which of the following is generally *not* a funding source for an entrepreneur's company?
   a. Sale of publicly traded stock
   b. Venture capital funds
   c. Public job-creation grants
   d. Family members and friends
3. Which of the following statements is true?
   a. Lower returns result from higher risk in a free market.
   b. Risk assessment protocols can be perfected.
   c. Risk is not a factor in investment decisions.
   d. Risk is the probability of a unfavorable outcome.

4. Which of the following statements is *not* true?
   a. The time value of money has a mathematical basis.
   b. The time value of money says that a dollar today is better than a dollar tomorrow.
   c. The time value of money is used to calculate payback periods.
   d. The time value of money shows how the value of money decreases over time.

5. Discounted cash flows _____ .
   a. are used for calculating the net present value
   b. do not account for the time value of money
   c. are weighted toward slower cash flows
   d. are not used for investment analysis

6. Which of the following statements is *not* true?
   a. The net present value estimates the value of your product today.
   b. A positive net present value demonstrates that the investment will make money.
   c. The net present value is used to compare various investment opportunities.
   d. The net present value does not require discounting back future cash flows.

7. Valuation is _____ .
   a. an exactly calculated value for your product
   b. an assessment that includes risk and the time value of money
   c. useless for investment decisions
   d. determined the same way for product managers and entrepreneurs

8. Internal rates of return _____ .
   a. are calculated from payback periods
   b. include external factors like inflation
   c. are highest when the product development cycle is short and sales are high
   d. represent the discount rate where the net present value is positive

9. Which of the following is a key concept in discounted cash flow analysis?
   a. It's better to wait for cash.
   b. You cannot estimate the value today of a cash stream tomorrow.
   c. Cash in is better than cash out.
   d. Money holds the same value forever.

10. IRRs are higher if _____ .
    a. the net present value cannot be calculated
    b. the product development cycle is short
    c. sales volumes do not compensate for product development
    d. cash inflows are generated sooner

2

IMPLEMENTATION: IT AIN'T OVER 'TIL IT'S OVER

The first half of this book set forth the building blocks for a product development plan in abstract terms; strategy and marketing define the high-level viewpoint. Intellectual property management supports strategy by creating sustainable competitive advantage, and a well-written plan is backed by a reasonable financial analysis and the knowledge that a clear value proposition motivates the projected revenue stream.

Part 2 addresses implementation challenges and shows you multiple examples of how top companies put theory into practice. Chapters 7 and 8 describe organizations involved in product development. Chapter 7 discusses how development groups fit into different types of companies and institutions and then reviews models for creating a strong organization through effective leadership and motivated teams. Chapter 8 describes fundamental project management tools as communication techniques and reviews how milestones are used on an industry-wide basis, as well as for an individual company.

Chapters 9 and 10 introduce the product trajectory, an offshoot of Michael Porter's value chain that emphasizes the role of design. This framework enables a straightforward identification of economical solutions to the challenges of design, fabrication, integration, and delivery. We will look at vertically integrated companies that manage all processes, from procurement of raw materials to delivery to the consumer, and then consider a number of outsourcing models.

Chapter 11 returns to the theme of marketing in the context of product launch. It describes the mechanics of innovation diffusion to explain how the target of a launch campaign differs from the object of a product with significant traction. It then discusses the elements of an advertising campaign and describes successful launches. Because launch success is strongly related to positioning and generating trust, the chapter also summarizes best practices in recalls.

In Chapter 12, you will learn how to wrap up a project through an effective postmortem process. This chapter integrates many of the book's lessons in the context of contemporary product development and points out trends in strategy, design, and changing customer relationships to better arm you in your battles.

Like Part 1, Part 2 identifies the role of risk analysis and mitigation in creating your plan. Furthermore, each chapter explicitly relates each topic back to the building blocks from Part 1 to show how a plan must be much more than a simple vision. All the elements are strongly interrelated.

While strategy and marketing are exciting and typically attract dreamy-eyed futurists, true innovators have mastered the economics of product fabrication and clearly understand every step involved in delivering value to a customer. Part 2 will appeal strongly to a real "doer" who wants to bring a vision to life.

7

ORGANIZATIONS

Organization charts and fancy titles count for
next to nothing.

—COLIN POWELL

Most businesses claim that their people are their greatest asset. Ha! How many executives really think about their employees in terms of returns or optimizing additional investment in this asset? In start-ups, it can be even more challenging if the staff consists mainly of technically gifted engineers who are uncomfortable with touchy-feely people skills. There is no question: people are by far the hardest asset to manage. But what's the alternative?

If you try to learn management from books, your chances of success are mixed at best. These books typically spew out tons of acronyms for psychological profile tools. While they may provide insight, they don't help much if you're starting a company with extra money from Mom or if you just got promoted to your first line management position. Furthermore, these tomes usually don't cover how organizational management simultaneously interacts with strategy, intellectual property, finance, or the other building blocks we discussed in Part 1.

Thus we'll approach this topic differently, starting with an introduction to the types of organizations that support product development. Then we'll talk about motivating your team through your inspiring leadership and by creating effective "followship." Finally, we'll discuss how organizational management impacts each basic business element.

THE BLUEPRINT: PRODUCT DEVELOPMENT GROUPS

How is product development organized inside a company? Logically, concepts come from either within or without, but someone has to support the ideation process. Should some groups import ideas from other organizations? Are there environments in which product development shouldn't take place?

There are spin-up, spin-in, and spin-out models. In spin-up activities, an internal group drives product development from the original concept to completion. Spin-in efforts import or integrate externally developed products. Spin-out is the reverse of spin-in; organizations with new applications transfer them to another entity to complete development.

Spin-Up: Internal Innovation

Internal innovation happens in companies all the time (hopefully), but it's often in an ad hoc way. How can you accelerate this process?

Let's look at Google as an example of an innovation mastermind. The company introduces products at a rapid-fire pace, bringing out more than 100 new products in 10 years thanks to its rapid, disciplined process of development and testing. The company uses various tactics to manage these processes, but we will address two key elements here (you can learn more about their management practices in the excellent *Harvard Business Review* article by Bala Iyer and Thomas Davenport[1]):

- **Mandatory innovation:** The company requires that technical staff members must spend as much as 20 percent of their time on new ideas. Even managers follow this scheme, allocating 20 percent of their time to projects related to the core business and an additional 10 percent to entirely new products. Performance reviews include this requirement, and additional corporate-level management exists to oversee how concepts developed this way transition into mainstream product development.

- **Flexible organization:** The organization has flexible reporting structures to review product concepts faster than would be possible through standard line management. The deep bench of talented developers accelerates the validation and verification process, generating quality product review without lengthy approval processes by going across the organization to other experts.

Both these techniques work best with highly trained and motivated individuals. In general, spin-up works most effectively when the company has extensive technical expertise and doesn't need to look elsewhere for concept reviews or improvement. Therefore, you need to hire extremely good people. Period. You can cover some of the same distance if you streamline approval processes, allowing review groups to coalesce as needed. (A similar technique is to create "Tiger Teams," internal groups tasked with intensive review of operations suffering from bottlenecks in product development.)

Spin-In: Acquisition of New Products

Some companies grow mainly by importing new concepts and even existing product lines. Entrepreneurs should appreciate this method, since it highlights the path to an exit by acquisition. How does an acquisitive company think? How does management integrate new products?

Cisco, the powerhouse behind much of the infrastructure of the digital age, has grown to a $15 billion behemoth by acquiring other companies, then introducing their products through existing distribution channels. In the 2000–2009 decade, Cisco led the list of corporations with the highest number of acquisitions by buying 50 companies,[2] roughly one acquisition every two months. Miraculously, Cisco does this while keeping a low turnover rate (8 percent) for employees of acquired companies—the same rate as for long-term employees.[3] What's its secret? Two processes:

- **Buddy system:** When Cisco completes an acquisition, its "buddy system" swaps some existing Cisco employees with those at the target company to ensure a smooth transition into a combined operation. In addition, Cisco appoints a senior manager from the acquired company to direct the manufacturing integration team so it is still led by a well-known and trusted figure.

- **Integration process analysis:** The Cisco team determines the integration needs in three areas—merging information systems, aligning current processes, and implementing ongoing methodologies. This integration effort aims to convert operations to Cisco's model in just 90 days. Cisco changes information systems to its own to reduce corporate overhead. In process alignment, management reviews the target supplier list and processes, seeking areas where quality and timely delivery can be improved as necessary and searching for outsourcing opportunities. Finally, the target company adopts methodologies such as Cisco's defect reduction procedures, forecasting techniques, and New Product Introduction process (discussed further in Chapter 8).

Effective spin-in thus combines the best of the shared resources, both in people and in processes. Small companies interested in being acquired by or working with a larger organization should invest the time necessary to generate a smooth working relationship.

Spin-Out: Creating a New Entity to Develop the Product

Spin-outs work for organizations, such as universities and research laboratories, where product development is inappropriate. To accelerate a technology's commercialization, the research organization licenses the property to a start-up company; some technology transfer offices may also use an intellectual property broker. Spinning out technologies from academic environments has several advantages for both the university and the new company:

- **Structured culture:** In a spin-out company, you can create a culture that is less laid-back than the typical university laboratory staffed by students who trickle in at noon to start their workday. (Unfortunately, management often does not seize this opportunity, and product development still lags; this is a key issue in many university spin-outs).
- **Development of a marketing philosophy:** Every successful business must maintain an intense focus on determining market trends, creating needs in prospective customers, and satisfying existing customers. By design, university research lacks this direction, which goes hand-in-hand with a more driven corporate culture.

- **Ability to raise money:** In a university, you cannot raise funds from private investors, but a start-up company is the perfect forum for this activity. Start-ups require some infrastructure in terms of corporate structure and accounting processes, but they have the ability to raise funds from government grant programs as well as from investors.

Spin-out also takes place in corporations where a newly developed product concept is not well aligned with the company's core marketing strategy or key markets of interest. As described in Chapter 1, Everett Rogers's *Diffusion of Innovations* discusses how Xerox ultimately spun out the original computer mouse to Apple because Xerox did not view it as a good fit with the company's focus on copies and images.[4]

CONCEPT

Product Development Organizations

Spin-up, spin-in, and *spin-out* development work best in different environments. Spin-up works best when internal technical staff is highly competent and the company seeks to maintain product development knowledge in-house. Companies growing by acquisition use spin-in processes to integrate people and systems. Universities and research organizations typically spin out their technologies, as do companies with new products that do not align with their core marketing strategy.

PEOPLE I: EFFECTIVE LEADERSHIP

Now that we have identified the types of organizations developing new products, we need to staff them from the top down. We'll discuss leadership, the ability to motivate others to execute their work, and what I call "followship"— programs that help employees motivate themselves. (Of course, none of these programs will work without the right people.)

U.S. Military: Centralized Command–Decentralized Execution

The military is obviously a great place to look for leadership models; it successfully creates a unified team from a diverse set of backgrounds and generates loyalty toward carefully selected leaders. Like all organizations, the armed forces undergo tremendous change in the process of upgrading to modern technologies and modifying the leadership toolbox to suit the current environment. In other words, generals now have different jobs than when the leaders of the American Revolution lined up farmers with muskets.

Today's military leaders have virtually complete visibility into real-time operations and are in a position to react nearly instantly to changes. (Doesn't this sound like modern business?) One new framework is centralized command–decentralized execution (CC-DE).[5] CC-DE management has two key features: centralized direction comes from top management, and responsibility and authority for specific actions is pushed down the chain of command. In practical terms, this means that the troops "get it" and are both capable and authorized to make effective decisions.

Although the term *CC-DE* isn't used frequently, we will see in Chapter 10 that some of today's most forward-thinking organizations, like the clothing manufacturer Zara, use this same philosophy to develop products rapidly. CC-DE works best if management can do the following:

- **Obtain rapid environmental measurements:** In business, this refers to obtaining market data frequently to detect trends and opportunities.
- **Exploit information architecture:** Simple tools like smartphones and Internet connections are used to distribute current data widely throughout the system.
- **Keep reactive systems ready:** Management continues to brainstorm product concepts so that exciting products are ready for new opportunities.
- **Nurture leadership capabilities:** At all levels of the organization, managers search for and develop those who command people's attention.
- **Keep communication lines open:** Free channels up and down the chain of command are maintained and nurtured.

When new information arrives, teams should interpret it efficiently and competently. Frankly, most entrepreneurs fail at this step because they do not analyze market intelligence objectively, nor do they change their direction in response to information received. A start-up's key asset is nimbleness, but most companies fail to take advantage and move quickly.

General Electric: Defining and Identifying Leaders

General Electric (GE) is legendary for its ability to identify, train, and grow leadership, with alumni often going on to CEO roles at Fortune 500 companies. How does this system work?

In addition to having the luxury and budget to recruit top people, the organization has clearly defined its requirements for good leadership. Which traits does the company seek? Steven Prokesch analyzed GE's leadership "wish list" in the *Harvard Business Review*:[6]

- **Deep expertise:** Loves learning and commands credibility based on experience
- **Clear thinker:** Seeks simple solutions to complex problems
- **Imaginative thinker:** Takes risk on people and ideas
- **Inclusive leader:** Respects others' contributions and builds loyalty
- **External focus:** Defines success through the customer's eyes

Although Prokesch didn't catalog the traits this way, this listing demonstrates a natural evolution to higher levels of leadership. Expertise will earn you early recognition and responsibility; the best folks reinvent their domain of interest every few years. Those with a deep understanding of the subject then develop the ability to find simple solutions to complex problems as clear thinkers, identifying and prioritizing the key levers driving a complex technical or business problem.

The next level marks a key difference in an innovator's path, because it starts to incorporate other people. Imaginative thinkers seek not just improvements for existing solutions, but entirely new ones. Because these people are willing to try new approaches, they become inclusive leaders as they generate excitement and build loyalty. Finally, the highest quality of leadership takes place when innovators develop external focus, defining success through customer satisfaction.

This probably sounds more like a Zen mind-set than a career path as it evolves from subject matter expert to leader, but you must learn how to develop insight in both the topic at hand and your customers' needs. Understanding just one of these is not enough.

Gore: Creating Guitar Strings in Your Spare Time

W. L. Gore & Associates—the maker of Gore-Tex fabrics, Glide dental floss, and many other products—is well known for its interesting management models. (In *The Tipping Point*, Malcolm Gladwell discussed the practice of separating groups when the head count exceeds 150.[7]) How does this corporation assign leadership responsibilities?

Simply put, it doesn't. Gore's informal training begins at hire, when new recruits are assigned "starting sponsors" rather than bosses and do not get standard job descriptions.[8] Instead, they are thrown onto teams to see if and how they can contribute. The organization does not have a formal chain of command; instead, leaders emerge simply by attracting talent to a project.

For instance, the top-selling acoustic guitar string, Elixir, began development when a Gore engineer working on his mountain bike coated the cables with a product similar to Gore-Tex. He started to think about other wires that require coating, eventually coming to guitar strings as a good application after he discussed it with a colleague. One by one, a team of nine people coalesced, working on the product in their spare time for three years until they needed corporate-level support to take it to market. Elixir now controls a leading 35 percent market share in guitar strings.

The Gore example demonstrates that although organizations don't need titles, they still need leaders. Gore's recruiting process may not include formal job descriptions, but the company still recruits with certain skill sets in mind. Clearly creativity and success must serve as stronger motivators than job titles.

IDEO: No Job Titles

The famed Silicon Valley design studio IDEO is consistently identified as one of the world's most creative companies. In fact, it has helped develop products for many innovative companies such as 3M, Hewlett-Packard, Avery Dennison, and others. We will look at its processes in more detail later, but right now let's study the company's organization.[9]

Like Gore, IDEO does not have job titles; instead, people organize themselves into teams for projects, and at completion, the teams are disbanded. Individuals can choose to work on one large project as principals or on as many as three to four as contributors; to be a principal, someone just has to be the first to be excited and committed. Consequently, peer pressure drives IDEO's performance more than organizational structure. Employees often work 50 to 60 hours a week trying to keep up with the rest of the team.

Management in flexible teams can be effective in environments where people are self-motivated and sensitive to their peers' level of effort. IDEO shows that great work does not require complicated organizational structures.

CONCEPT

Leadership Models

Structured organizations tend to have clearly articulated models for leadership. The U.S. military has developed centralized command–decentralized execution for environments where operations are fairly transparent and everyone can make decisions in real time. General Electric has generated its own list of desirable leadership traits. On the other hand, Gore and IDEO demonstrate how to nurture leadership organically, relying on people to organize themselves into teams.

PEOPLE II: INSPIRING FOLLOWSHIP

So far we have discussed leadership models. But your soup may not need more chefs; you need dedicated workers to actually execute your bold, creative plan developed in the first half of this book. How do you foster a culture that capitalizes on everyone's capabilities? Many innovative companies have dynamic processes that bring out the best in the entire workforce and inspire *followship*, my term for the other half of the leader relationship. (Yes, I know that technically it should be *followership*, but I think this sounds better.)

Followship happens when people with self-discipline and common sense are empowered to keep an organization on track without requiring constant daily input from senior management. To create followship, management must trust its employees to manage their own time and activities, believing that it will be in the company's best interests. Leaders typically demonstrate this trust through policies that give employees the freedom to make the right decisions and form effective teams.

Of course, it's easier to bring out the best if you hire the best. But you can optimize any group's performance with techniques that are easy to implement and give substantial payoffs.

Nordstrom: Rule Number One

Retail leader Nordstrom has long enjoyed a strong reputation for providing phenomenal customer service. How does the corporation's management create a history of excellence when it is hard to quantify good service?

It is apocryphal that the original Nordstrom employee handbook was a single index card stating: "Nordstrom's Rule #1: Use good judgment in all situations. There will be no additional rule."[10] Although the handbook has evolved with the company's growth, the principle remains intact and expresses the military CC-DE model discussed earlier. Nordstrom urges its troops to be wise; how hard is that? Evidently, it's quite hard: customer service continues to be a key source of competitive advantage for the store.

Gore and 3M: Mandatory Creativity

Several innovative organizations encourage or require that employees spend a fraction of their time on problems that are not central to the core business. An earlier section described how Gore entered—and then dominated—the market for acoustic guitar strings after an enterprising employee discovered a coating for bicycle cables. The time to work on that discovery came from Gore's policy that encourages staff to spend 10 percent of their time on new ideas.

Even sticky notes were born this way. Manufacturer 3M has been innovating for more than a century. The company proudly advertises its "bootlegging" policy in marketing materials, in which it encourages technical staff to spend up to 15 percent of their time on projects of their own choosing.[11]

It may seem counterintuitive to require creativity, but such demands generate an entirely different culture. Consider the difference between an organization whose staff spend 20 percent of their time on new projects versus an organization where 20 percent of the staff spend all their time racking their brains for new ideas. Which organization sounds like more fun?

Nucor: Incentivizing the Team

Innovators may think that steel manufacturers are boring and static companies, but think again: Nucor has thrived through nearly 50 years of change in the steel industry, growing at about 15 percent annually (until the financial crisis of 2008). The company has developed key organizational innovations that enabled it to survive and grow consistently.[12]

Decentralized Management

Remarkably, the company has only four management layers:

- Chairman/vice chairman/president
- Vice president/plant general manager
- Department manager
- Supervisor

That's it—no executive vice president, senior vice president, director, or anything else. General managers have considerable autonomy and run their plants as independent businesses. This relatively flat structure creates less jockeying for power and more collaboration.

Group Incentive Plan

Nucor offers bonuses for the performance of groups of 25 to 40 people rather than for individual output. This incentive bonus has no upper cap. Bonuses reflect not just quality levels and output quantity, but also attendance and tardiness standards. Can you imagine how you would feel if 39 of your coworkers lost their bonuses because you were a little late for work?

You don't have to worry that equipment failure may put the bonus out of reach; maintenance personnel manning all shifts participate in the same plan, with no bonus paid if equipment fails. Everyone in the company must deliver thanks to similar incentive plans for corporate level management and administrative personnel, all based on return on assets. Weekly outputs and bonus levels are displayed publicly at the factory entrance.

Cost-Saving Measures

Admirably, management refuses to conduct layoffs in recessionary periods; even as recently as 2009, Nucor reduced its work week instead.[13] This attitude creates such a positive environment that the company is not unionized; workers simply don't feel the need for a third party in order to be heard by management.

Can you, as an innovator, adopt all these practices? Perhaps not; the Nucor model may not work in all industries or even all steel companies. But these methods are certainly worth considering as ways to convert groups into teams.

CONCEPT

Followship Models

Simply put, creative organizations typically trust their employees. This confidence appears in simple guidelines, such as Nordstrom's Rule Number One, or through added flexibility in reporting structures. Companies also show their faith in employees by allocating a large amount of time to activities that are not part of the core business. Finally, creative incentive programs can motivate better teamwork, especially if management distributes rewards equitably throughout the organization.

ORGANIZATION AND BUSINESS BUILDING BLOCKS

To design a creative product, you need to design a creative organization. Attract imaginative people to a supportive structure. The right configuration of people and titles will help you maximize the chances of product success. Here we will examine each of the fundamental business strategic elements to see how they interact with the organizational framework and layers.

Strategy

To paraphrase Jim Collins's groundbreaking work in *Good to Great*, even average companies can excel when a strong leader steps in and "gets the right people on the bus, then decides where the bus is headed."[14] If you put good people in a room with a whiteboard, they will figure out an effective strategy.

Hire people who fit in with your culture. If you're building a relatively flat organization like Nucor, you don't want to hire people who are motivated by business cards with fancy titles. If your group is highly structured, then you need employees who are sensitive to the dynamics of navigating complex organizations.

Marketing

Organizational structure affects marketing because every employee is a member of your sales force. Anyone who answers the phone, generates an invoice, or talks to an investor is a face of your company. Hire someone only after asking yourself during an interview, "Do I want this person to represent my company?" Nordstrom may have only one simple rule, but careful hiring processes ensure that the company doesn't place its strong reputation in the wrong hands.

Intellectual Property

You cannot develop intellectual property without talent in the proverbial trenches. It takes a tremendous amount of ingenuity and daily observation to develop a product concept—and line managers are often so busy putting out fires that they don't have the time or patience for this level of creativity. (For that reason, innovators in engineering organizations dread being tapped to lead a group.)

Thus, creating followship is absolutely critical for most organizations. Treat engineers well, and your patent portfolio will follow. On the other hand, if you squander this opportunity and select uninspired people whose biggest concern is keeping their jobs—and there are plenty of these folks—you will find that you won't last long in the marketplace.

Funding

Good money follows good people. "Penny-wise and pound-foolish" hiring attitudes form mediocre companies with terrible products. Firing the wrong person is always more expensive than spending a little more time on hiring, so hire with care.

If you are spinning out your technology into a new company, seek employees who are ready to be in a company rather than a country club and incentivize them with stock options. Culture mismatch is a common reason for poor outcomes in university technology transfer. Finally, once you have the right people on board, invest in ongoing training for your employees so they can contribute more effectively to your plans.

Funding is also strongly affected by spin-up and spin-out decisions, because both are intimately linked to decisions regarding licensing technology versus building it yourself. The funding needs are much higher for spin-up processes, as well as for manufacturing. We will cover this in more detail in Chapters 10 and 11.

HINT

Organization and Fundamental Business Elements
Strong people develop good strategies as they think through a business's opportunities, so strategy and organization cannot be divorced. Since everyone is part of your sales force, organization and marketing go hand in hand. Intellectual property development only takes place in environments that support creative thinking and novel applications. Finally, funding follows people with the right background and capabilities.

HINT

Organization and Service Providers
Service providers also need to match employee values with organizational culture—ask any Arthur Anderson alumnus who was sorry to see the company collapse in the Enron scandal. Carefully consider how you will grow, keeping in mind that anyone who answers the phone or handles accounts receivable represents your company.

Although they do not generally face spin-in and spin-out decisions, service firms do grow by either hiring or acquisitions, depending on whether they just want to add capacity or want a new clientele. Both can be effective strategies.

KEYS TO SUCCESS

Good people can make great products—if they are organized to do so. Creative cultures and efficient execution don't happen accidentally. Like children and tomato plants, organizations grow with a mind of their own and require careful supervision to achieve a positive outcome.

Creative product development requires three ingredients: a favorable structure, effective leaders, and committed followers. The appropriate organizational structure—spin-in, spin-out, or spin-up—varies with the parent company and depends on its internal technical resources and its capability to market efficiently.

Once you identify the right format for your company, you need to staff it with the right people. Some leadership models thrive in highly structured environments, while others achieve employee loyalty through more organic processes. In either situation, leaders tend to stand out; you need to find them. Maintain loyalty in your people by treating them with respect and rewarding them for effective teamwork. Excited employees create exciting products.

George McGovern once observed, "The longer the title, the less important the job." Good product development requires organizations that nurture creativity rather than inflating egos.

Chapter Quiz

1. **Which of the following statements is *not* true?**
   a. An organization can deliberately seek a specific set of leadership traits.
   b. Rapidly changing environments can nurture leadership to enable effective decision making in real time.
   c. People require formal leadership titles to establish and nurture teamwork.
   d. Leadership and followership require equal attention to create an effective organization.
2. **Keys to effective spin-in include _____ .**
   a. considering integration needs in multiple areas
   b. keeping the target organization separate from the acquirer
   c. placing someone from the acquiring company in the lead integration role
   d. keeping transition costs low by leaving the target's operations alone

3. **Which of the following statements is *not* true?**
   a. Strategy and organization are linked through good people.
   b. Organizational development is not linked to funding development.
   c. Intellectual property management is linked to environments supporting clear and creative thinking.
   d. Organizations and marketing are linked because everyone is a member of your sales force.

4. **Organizations with strong fellowship models typically _____ .**
   a. require adherence to formal reporting structures without any leeway
   b. must have strong individual incentive programs to keep internal competition high
   c. demonstrate faith in their employees through creative initiatives
   d. require all employees to focus exclusively on the company's core business

5. **Which of the following is *not* an element of centralized command–decentralized execution models?**
   a. Measurements can be obtained rapidly.
   b. Information architecture can be readily exploited for fast communication.
   c. Leadership is taken seriously and nurtured.
   d. Levels of command are isolated from one another.

6. **Which of the following is *not* a model for product development?**
   a. Spin-up
   b. Spin-in
   c. Spin-out
   d. Spin-down

7. **Which of the following statements is true?**
   a. Quality reviews can be generated by going across, not just up, an organization.
   b. Innovation cannot be mandatory because you can't be creative on demand.
   c. Fast innovation requires that concepts move rapidly through standard line management.
   d. Managers have no time for thinking about new products.

8. **Which of the following is *not* an element of GE's leadership model?**
   a. Deep expertise: Loves learning
   b. Internal focus: Defines success internally
   c. Clear thinker: Seeks simple solutions
   d. Imaginative thinker: Takes risk

9. **University spin-outs do *not* benefit from a focus on _____ .**
   a. recruiting students
   b. raising money

    c.   a structured culture

    d.   marketing products

10. Which of the following statements is *not* true for service providers?

    a.   They can grow by adding capability or clientele.

    b.   Everyone in the organization represents the company.

    c.   Service firms often face spin-in and spin-out decisions.

    d.   Employee values and organizational culture must be aligned.

C H A P T E R

MILESTONES

It's when ordinary people rise above the expecta-
tions and seize the opportunity that milestones truly
are reached.

—MIKE HUCKABEE

I f organizational management answers the question of who, then project management methodology offers the what, where, and when. (Strategy addresses the why.) Project management complements organizational development in meeting company milestones.

Unlike strategy and marketing, milestones sound decidedly un-sexy. Most people enjoy talking about visionary companies or cool advertising concepts, but milestones start to sound like hard work. The only way the topic could sound less appealing is if we called it "project management"—thus the chapter title.

Milestones are measurable goals, while project management is the method used to communicate a team's progress in meeting its milestones. In this chapter, we'll examine the nuts and bolts of project management and learn about both journey and destination planning models from industry.

Just as we mark "turning 40" rather than "getting older," milestones must represent quantifiable achievements. "Becoming the most innovative company in the world" is not good enough, because of there is no definition of "most innovative." Use "being first to market," "finishing our beta version," and other objectively defined terms.

Part 1 of this book described the key function of management as evaluating and mitigating risk. In this spirit, project management and milestone review are critical activities because they reveal and address sources of risk.

CONCEPT

Milestones and Project Management

Milestones are measurable goals. *Project management* is the method used to communicate a team's progress in meeting its milestones.

THE RESOURCE TRIANGLE

Ruthless prioritization lies at the heart of good execution. On any given day, you could probably do 10 different things; you might call potential customers, work closely with your intellectual property attorney, or evaluate financing options. Which activity is your highest priority? How do you meet your goals?

Your resource triangle has three components: money, time, and people. Even though many people think they need money most, it is actually the least critical resource, because all money is the same and you can always generate more. Time is trickier, because a minute gone is gone; you can't make any more. People are by far the most sensitive part of your resource triangle.

Carefully allocating your resources allows you to manage your risk. Think of them as investments in a portfolio; spending on one of these resources should generate more of another one, as shown conceptually in Figure 8-1. Hiring the right people generates more revenues. Good employees also generate more time for you to look for new opportunities. Automating processes saves employee expenses.

CONCEPT

The Resource Triangle

Your *resource triangle* consists of money, time, and people. You must use them appropriately to manage your risk.

Figure 8-1 The Resource Triangle Consists of Money, Time, and People

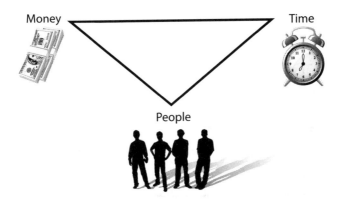

COST PROFILES AND RISK REDUCTION

In product development, bringing a technology to maturity costs more as you approach readiness. A typical curve showing how costs change over time, or cost profile, is shown in Figure 8-2.

The earliest development stage is cheap, because it is usually a proof of concept. Although few innovators do it, you should invest in marketing research at this early stage, because the results will tell you whether it makes sense to proceed or not. Many innovators invest in too much product development before discovering that the market doesn't warrant that degree of spending; this lesson has cost companies untold millions. Carry out risk assessment and reduction throughout the product development process before you incur further costs.

CONCEPT

Cost Profiles
Product development typically gets progressively more expensive as you get closer to the market. The shape of this curve is the *cost profile*.

Figure 8-2   A Typical Cost Profile

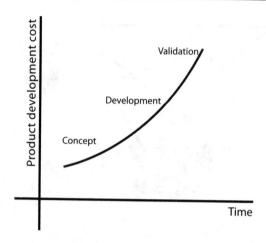

GANTT CHARTS

Although many project management planning tools exist, the Gantt chart (named after Henry Gantt) is by far the most common because it usually specifies the tasks and timing for project activities, as shown in Figure 8-3. This is an extremely useful tool in showing a team how its activities overlap and mesh together. For management use, Gantt charts may also include projected spending levels to show how funding needs change over time.

CONCEPT

Gantt Charts

A *Gantt chart* is the most commonly used project management tool. It visually indicates the tasks and timing for project activities and may also include resource allocation.

Figure 8-3   A Schematic for a Gantt Chart

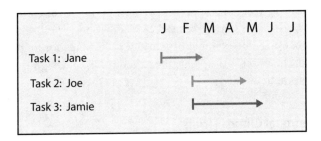

GO/NO-GO DECISION

Gantt charts and progress assessments should help you make decisions, although rookie innovators tend to think of them as mindless exercises for their bosses. This is not so! Comparing progress to a Gantt chart helps pinpoint where a development effort is going astray—and even more important, when to shut it down. This is known as a go/no-go decision.

This "no" may seem very expensive because of the investment you have already made; naturally, you don't want to throw good money after bad. However, the costs of continuing are usually much worse. Get used to the go/no-go lingo if you are going to work in product development or capital allocation.

CONCEPT

Go/No-Go Decisions
Progress toward milestones and Gantt charts are key tools for making *go/no-go decisions* about continuing or reworking a project.

To be poetic, you can use either the journey or the destination as the milestone marker. That is, you can label the milestones by either the stage (such as "evaluate feasibility") or the product of that stage ("feasibility analysis"). While this may seem like a subtle distinction, it determines how you communicate your progress to investors and customers. Neither is right or wrong; they just represent different perspectives.

JOURNEY MILESTONES

Journey milestones describe project activities at a given time. The pharmaceutical industry uses this approach in earning approval from the Food and Drug Administration (FDA) to market medications. We'll look at the clinical trial process as an example of journey milestones for an entire industry, then review the process at IDEO, the Silicon Valley design firm, to see how it works in practice.

Pharmaceutical Clinical Trials

Modern advances in molecular biology have revolutionized drug development and the pharmaceutical industry. As you can imagine, novel compounds undergo extensive testing to assess their toxicity and effectiveness. In fact, it costs an average of about 12 years and $500 million (including failed drugs and opportunity costs) to bring a new drug to market.[1]

The National Institutes of Health (NIH) and the FDA have developed a typical "journey" scheme that identifies each phase by the activities taking place. Let's see what happens after animal and laboratory trials to understand a good journey destination system, as shown in Figure 8-4.

Figure 8-4   Journey Milestones for Pharmaceutical Clinical Trials

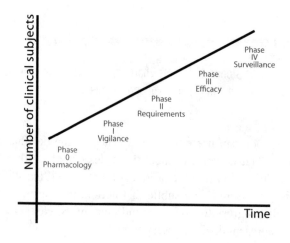

- **Phase 0—Pharmacology:** Assess how the body processes the drug and how the drug works in the body with 10 to 15 subjects.
- **Phase I—Vigilance:** Assess safety and tolerability with tests of 20 to 100 subjects.
- **Phase II—Requirements:** Continue safety tests and determine effectiveness with 20 to 300 subjects. This is the phase where drugs most commonly fail because they don't work as planned or have toxic effects.
- **Phase III—Efficacy:** Compare the drug efficacy to the state of the art with 300 to 3,000 subjects, often in parallel with the approval process.
- **Phase IV—Surveillance:** Continue ongoing studies after FDA permission is granted. In some cases this leads to drugs being recalled, such as Merck's 2004 recall of the painkiller Vioxx.

The increasing number of subjects in each step agrees well with the idea that testing gets more expensive as you get closer to market. Imagine what happens if you discover the problems at the end; the Vioxx withdrawal from the marketplace was estimated to cost as much as $2 billion.[2] Here, the go/no-go decision happened far too late (that is, not at all), creating a remarkably expensive failed product.

IDEO: A Phase Dedicated to Understanding the Client

The famous Silicon Valley design firm IDEO was introduced in Chapter 7, and we'll continue studying it in Chapter 9. Right now we'll look to the company to answer this question: how do you take an inherently chaotic process—namely, design—and impose the disciplined mind-set of project management?

Although we saw in Chapter 7 that the organization is fluid, the process has a clear structure. This gives the firm a template for communicating with large manufacturing companies that are organized more formally. The steps in an IDEO design project are as follows:[3]

- **Phase 0—Understand/observe:** Understand the client's needs
- **Phase I—Visualize/realize:** Choose a direction for design
- **Phase II—Evaluate/refine:** Refine design prototypes and functional prototypes

- **Phase III—Implement detailed engineering:** Finish the design
- **Phase IV—Implement manufacturing liaison:** Release the design to manufacturing

Again, the process gets more expensive as the team approaches the finish line; prototyping (Phase II) requires more investment than understanding clients' needs (Phase 0). We will discuss the details of the prototype process in Chapter 9.

DESTINATION MILESTONES

Another way of thinking about product development is to focus on the destination instead of the journey. Some people and groups, especially highly structured groups, work better by thinking about the end game.

Technology Readiness Levels

The U.S. aerospace and defense industry makes extensive use of a scheme called Technology Readiness Levels (TRLs),[4] shown in Figure 8-5, to objec-

Figure 8-5 Technology Readiness Levels Used in the United States Aerospace and Defense Industries

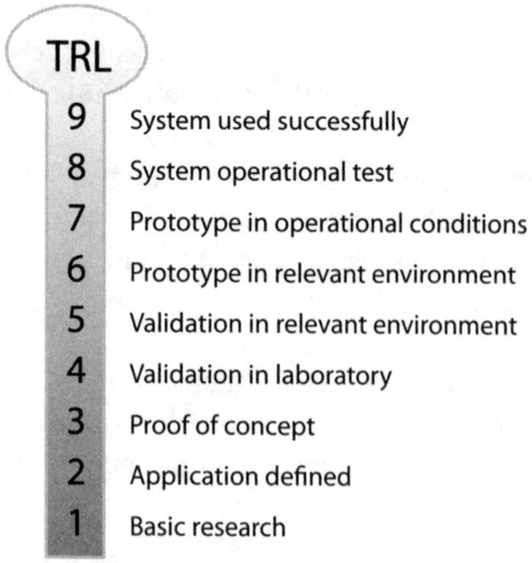

TRL	
9	System used successfully
8	System operational test
7	Prototype in operational conditions
6	Prototype in relevant environment
5	Validation in relevant environment
4	Validation in laboratory
3	Proof of concept
2	Application defined
1	Basic research

tively assess technology maturity. Much as the NIH and FDA requirements are relatively easy to find in public documents and on websites, the National Aeronautics and Space Administration (NASA) and the Department of Defense both make this information readily available. It's a great way to make apples-to-apples comparisons.

Once again we see that achieving early progress—namely, low TRL levels—is cheap, consisting of observing basic principles and formulating application concepts. Later progress becomes expensive because it entails rigorous testing, which requires the collection of statistically relevant sample sizes. At NASA, new technologies may not be integrated into flight projects (real spacecraft) unless they reach TRL 6 early enough to participate in testing; as you can imagine, this takes place long before launch.

You need to think the same way if your product development is geared toward capital equipment, because it likely needs to be integrated into another system, which requires further review. The sales cycle to include your new part in integrated systems for business-to-business customers thus gets longer. Bottom line: it can easily take two or three years from the time your application reaches maturity to when it reaches the market and generates revenues.

HINT

University Technology Transfer and TRL Levels
Why does the university technology transfer process have uneven success? One problem stems from the fact that universities typically patent technologies at approximately TRL 4, after demonstrating proof of concept through breadboard experiments. However, commercialization usually calls for performance in a relevant environment, which means getting to TRL 6. With university technology transfer, start-ups must close the gap between TRL 4 and TRL 6—and this is expensive.

Cisco: Commitment to Commitment

As we discussed in Chapter 7, Cisco completes an acquisition about once every two months. The company therefore closely links its product development process with efficient integration of acquisition targets. The new product introduction process at Cisco has several key milestones corresponding to the "destination" review that precedes the go/no-go decision at each step:[5]

- **Concept commit:** Design team brainstorms concepts.
- **Execute commit:** Multidisciplinary team (finance, manufacturing, and design) agrees on design specifications and target dates.
- **Design for manufacturability:** Manufacturing team reviews prototype.
- **Technical readiness review:** Manufacturing team estimates yields and quality metrics.
- **Orderability:** Manufacturing and distribution team estimates targeted ship date and volume.
- **First customer shipment:** Sales and manufacturing teams add item to price list.
- **Time to quality and volume:** Manufacturing team prepares for production.
- **Postproduction assessment:** Entire team regroups for lessons learned.

Chapter 12 will discuss the role of the last step, the postlaunch "lessons learned" session. However, this list should guide you in creating appropriate milestones. Your goal should be to identify and solve problems that would cause you to throw good money after bad.

MILESTONES AND BUSINESS BUILDING BLOCKS

When well executed, project management and milestone definition integrate the company's different functions. On the other hand, when they're not well done, you end up creating a funny comic strip like *Dilbert*. How do you serve as a get-it-done leader instead of the proverbial pointy-headed boss?

Strategy

Often innovators are distracted by many product concepts when technologies have multiple applications. This can grow into an expensive problem as precious resources are allocated to too many development projects.

Chapter 2 defined *strategy* as the process of aligning the company's actions with its vision. Defining milestones forces you to convert your strategic vision into quantifiable achievements at all organizational levels. For instance, at the top level, the goal may be "grow revenues by 10 percent"; at the sales level, this may take the form of "obtain five new customers" or "sell 10 percent more to existing customers."

Innovators sometimes don't like these discussions because it leads to a potentially uncomfortable "put your money where your mouth is" moment—and because they see it is more boring than the creative brainstorming process. Unfortunately, procrastinating on this conversation will convince investors or senior management to put their money elsewhere.

Marketing

Milestones link closely with marketing plans; in fact, a marketing plan should basically consist of a Gantt chart marking key customer "drop-dead dates." For instance, a company developing a new toy or product for Christmas has to complete its development and sales cycle by the spring in order to ship in a timely fashion. Similar issues can affect service providers; one example is data processing companies in the oil industry, which must complete their analyses in time for the drilling season. Accountants also must prepare their new products long before April 15 each year.

Include trade shows and industry conferences in a marketing Gantt plan. Trade shows are invaluable opportunities to "walk the floor" and see industry trends. Scientific conferences are even more important in technology-rich industries; both venues have the added benefit of providing chances to find good people to steal from other companies. (Don't tell anyone I said that.)

Intellectual Property

The development of intellectual property happens so early in the product life cycle that it often precedes the level of planning requiring Gantt charts and similar tools. However, strategic planning experts know that you must keep feeding the fire. Thus, product road maps—modified Gantt charts describing a schedule for new products to be released—are most likely to anticipate intellectual property activities, such as dates for new patents to be filed or for older ones to expire (a common concern in pharmaceutical companies).

Intellectual property protection granted by the government typically happens on an extended review schedule; missing these deadlines can create expensive or unrecoverable mistakes. This makes it imperative for entrepreneurs to closely monitor the calendar associated with filing applications.

Products that are further along in development have different considerations, such as when to file trademarks in connection with launch programs.

Funding

In today's environment, establishing and meeting reasonable milestones is a critical element to establishing credibility for financing your project. Funding in tranches, or installments, allows both public and private funding sources to mitigate risk by waiting to see how you perform. The mechanics of this process differs between grant agencies and private investors, but they share the same objective of ensuring that you are on track without putting all the money at risk at the outset. Some key notes about the process are:

• **Public funding sources:** Government grants usually require a research plan as part of the grant submission process. Many companies struggle with this, but it is critical because review panels look for plans with sensible milestones. Funded projects must demonstrate their progress via quarterly reports and annual review presentations to obtain the next installment.

• **Private funding sources:** Private investors may offer their funding in tranches, with each payment based on achievement of certain objectives. Other deals may be structured with valuation (that is, share price) determined by how well the company meets revenue goals. Frankly, if more investors followed this method, more companies would be fairly valued, particularly start-ups, where the valuation is difficult to estimate; however, this approach is more complicated and can be daunting to many investors and entrepreneurs alike.

HINT

Milestones and Fundamental Business Elements
The process of setting and meeting milestones describes your progress in converting your strategic vision into quantifiable achievements. In marketing, customer needs that are tied to calendars, such as planning for Christmas in retail sectors, impact your own milestones and timing. Intellectual property protection often involves complex schedules and is thus monitored through a project management technique, as are marketing calendars with trade shows, conferences, and related activities. Finance-related milestones include meeting certain objectives to receive tranches, or installments, of the promised funding.

Milestones and Service Providers

Milestones affect service providers as well if they are coordinating the efforts of multiple people. Like manufacturing companies, service companies that follow a strategy must tie their daily activities to their overarching objective. In addition, service providers effectively need to understand the schedules of their clients' customers, such as a consultant serving an aerospace contractor who needs to meet deadlines associated with the government's fiscal year. Service providers may find that they are maintaining multiple calendars associated with the varying trade show schedules, fiscal year start dates, and other dates associated with their clients' needs.

KEYS TO SUCCESS

The rubber meets the proverbial road when you begin to set milestones. Your toolbox includes understanding and allocating the resource triangle of money, time, and people. You should develop both a cost profile to show how the total development cost grows over time and a Gantt chart to show the schedule for meeting your goals.

There are two ways of thinking about your plan: journey milestones, in which you describe the activity taking place at each stage, and destination milestones, in which each activity ends with a review that enables you to decide whether to rescope or terminate the project. Every project should include gates where you can make go/no-go decisions.

Walt Disney once said, "Of all the things I've done, the most vital is coordinating the talents of those who work for us and pointing them toward a certain goal." Think about that the next time someone tells you that you have a Mickey Mouse project plan.

Chapter Quiz

1. Destination milestones _____ .
   a. describe the final review at each level
   b. are used only at the company-wide level
   c. are not useful in structured groups
   d. are better to inspire followship
2. Why is milestone development important for funding your project?
   a. It is only used for private investors and thus maintains confidentiality.
   b. It forces the funding group to finance the entire project at once.
   c. It keeps proprietary development protected from government review panels.
   d. It allows your source to manage risk.
3. Tranches are:
   a. Investor reviews
   b. Team discussions
   c. Funding installments
   d. Project stages
4. Milestone definition helps marketing plans because it _____ .
   a. focuses only on creative activities
   b. takes place independently of customer needs, preventing distraction
   c. can include trade shows, scientific conferences, and other events
   d. does not link with other company activities
5. Which of the following is *not* a component of the resource triangle?
   a. Money
   b. Strategy
   c. People
   d. Time
6. The cost profile is the curve describing _____ .
   a. cash flow once the product is in the market
   b. the increase in value as you get closer to acquisition
   c. the changing value of money with time
   d. the increase in development costs as you get closer to the market
7. Milestones are _____ .
   a. measurable goals
   b. value propositions
   c. communication methods
   d. organizational models

8. Which of the following is *not* part of a Gantt chart?
   a. Tasks
   b. Intellectual property
   c. Timing
   d. Resources
9. Journey milestones _____ .
   a. are not useful for organizations using Gantt charts
   b. constrain creativity in large organizations
   c. describe project activities at a given time
   d. are only useful at the industry-wide level
10. Why is milestone definition useful in developing a strategy?
   a. It frees innovation from time constraints.
   b. It does not constrain leadership by quantifying goals.
   c. It creates direction for all organizational levels.
   d. It can be delayed indefinitely.

C H A P T E R

9

DESIGN

Design is how it works.

—STEVE JOBS

A t last, design! You have probably been nurturing an image of your product for a long time and are ready to finally make your vision a reality. Perhaps your design is so clear that you don't even need this chapter; entrepreneur-visionaries may be especially quick to skip this section. On the other hand, managers at large organizations may find that they are looking for ways to reinvigorate their product design teams and need new ideas.

Product design is the process of analyzing a product's required specifications, prioritizing the associated functional elements, and integrating them into a physical package. Design reflects and advertises your sensibilities and priorities; considerations include superficial elements, such as car ornaments, as well as key functionality, such as the menu on an iPod screen.

CONCEPT

Design

Product *design* is the process of analyzing a product's required specifications, prioritizing the associated functional elements, and integrating them into a physical package.

This chapter is not a tutorial in elements of color theory or architecture. Instead, it will introduce you to the design process at many large organizations. The chapter is separated into three main sections. The first describes the design philosophies at several leading organizations and outlines their methodologies. The second describes how "rephrasing the question" opens more possibilities for game-changing innovation. Finally, the third describes how two leaders in environmental stewardship integrate their responsibilities with design.

PRODUCT TRACK

To understand assembly and delivery, we can follow Michael Porter's classic analysis from the book *Competitive Advantage* in visualizing a business as a chain of activities leading to delivery of an item or a service to a satisfied customer. The analysis begins with unfinished parts and ends in a finished product; the operations are supported by a corporate infrastructure, such as finance and human relations. This powerful value chain concept describes how a company delivers value to a customer; a similar analysis for manufacturing environments is known as "value chain mapping."

Because design is a key component in product development, we will take the general concept of moving from unfinished parts to a completed product, add the value of the design process, and call it the *product track*. This track does not include the supporting infrastructure, concentrating instead on the flow of activity from concept to delivered product. It is appropriate for goods, software, and services and is particularly powerful in looking for outsourcing opportunities. As shown in Figure 9-1, the product track has four steps: design, fabrication, integration, and delivery.

Figure 9-1 The Product Track Consists of Design, Fabrication, Integration, and Delivery. Each Step Adds Value, but Each Step Can Also Be Outsourced.

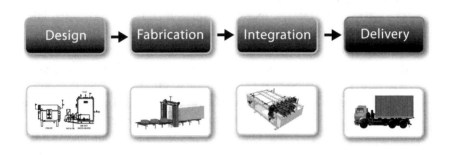

CONCEPT

Product Track
The *product track* consists of design, fabrication, integration, and delivery.

BUSINESS RELATIONSHIPS IN DESIGN AND MANUFACTURING

The electronics manufacturing services (EMS) industry virtually created a global outsourcing model in response to the personal computer revolution of the 1970s. The EMS methods for allocating the product track tasks have evolved, percolating into other industries where goods or even intellectual property can be shipped in their completed form in a cost-efficient fashion.

This way of allocating tasks introduced us to new models and associated terminology revolving around the original equipment manufacturer (OEM),[1] defined as the company branding the product and in direct contact with the marketplace. (Note that while other terms and definitions exist, we will follow those used by the EMS industry.) OEMs may outsource design and/or manufacturing under one of the following engagement models:

- **Retaining a contract design service firm:** In this model, the OEM hires another company to guide design but retains the intellectual property and design ownership. IDEO is an example of a contract design service firm.

- **Partnering with a contract design and manufacturing (CDM) firm:** The OEM and CDM partner on the design and jointly own the intellectual property. Because the CDM manufactures the product, it can optimize the design for ease of manufacturing, while the OEM's participation in design accelerates market acceptance because the OEM retains the responsibility for sales and marketing.
- **Hiring an original design manufacturer (ODM):** In this model, the ODM designs, builds, ships, and services the product and retains the intellectual property. The OEM specifies the design look and the user interface. ODMs can sell the same product to multiple OEMs that introduce new products rapidly because they focus only on sales and marketing activities.

The intellectual property ownership for each of these relationships is summarized in Table 9-1.

Table 9-1 Contract Manufacturing Relationships and Intellectual Property Ownership

Designer	IP Ownership
Contract firm	OEM
CDM	Shared with OEM
ODM	ODM

OEM = original equipment manufacturer; CDM = contract design and manufacturing firm; ODM = original design manufacturer.

CONCEPT

Business Relationships with Design and Manufacturing Companies
Original equipment manufacturers may have several types of relationships with other design and manufacturing companies. *Contract design firms* assist with design, leaving the intellectual property with the OEM, whereas *contract design*

and manufacturing firms may share the intellectual property with the OEM. *Original design and manufacturing companies* both design and manufacture components for many OEMs.

DESIGN PROCESSES: AN ORDERLY MESS

Design has two key elements: philosophy and methodology. Philosophy addresses how a company views meeting customer needs and reflects artistic or technical sensibilities. Methodology describes the daily implementation and tells a manager how to go about including the philosophy in everyday decision making.

IDEO: Rough, Ready, and Right

As mentioned in earlier chapters, the Silicon Valley design firm IDEO is a world-renowned creative force and works closely with other major global innovators.[2] IDEO's designs have been used in products as far-ranging as the Microsoft mouse and a transporter used for kidney transplants. How does this organization cover so much ground?

• **Philosophy:** IDEO's design process is geared toward "concurrent engineering"—designing products that are both esthetically pleasing and technically competent. This is obviously not trivial for complex products.
• **Methodology:** The company's Rough, Ready, and Right approach states that a prototype may be quick and dirty in some ways if it accurately reflects the key design elements under discussion. IDEO believes strongly that prototypes are necessary in order to communicate with users, customers, marketers, and internal partners, and it typically generates many—sometimes on a daily basis—in the course of product design. This process maintains tight control on both the artistic elements and the functionality.

I love the idea of Rough, Ready, and Right, even in writing or generating presentations. People complaining of writer's block often get stuck on such questions as whether it's worthwhile to put a bullet point on a presentation slide unless it is absolutely perfect. You can move ahead much faster if you look at intermediate versions, leaving the wordsmithing until the very end. Rough, Ready, and Right has a number of applications.

MINICASE

IDEO'S Brainstorming Rules
To maintain a tight loop between prototypes and concept improvements, IDEO conducts frequent and effective brainstorming sessions, eliminating the guesswork about the response to a proposed element. To optimize the sessions' success and participants' time, the company has implemented a set of rules combining rapid ideation with focus and courtesy:

- Include about eight people to have critical mass in a small group setting.
- Generate as many ideas as possible.
- Encourage wild ideas.
- Build on others' ideas.
- Focus on the topic at hand.
- Take turns speaking.
- Defer judgment so that you don't interrupt the stream of ideas.
- Sketch your ideas where possible.

Samsung: Yin and Yang

In the last decade, Samsung Electronics has met an ambitious set of goals, transforming itself from a manufacturer of commodity electronics to an award-winning, innovative organization with global reach.[3] To support this transformation, the company created seven design centers around the world and 17 research and development centers that develop products in three-year cycles. What is the company's inspiration, and how did it revamp itself?

   • **Philosophy:** Samsung derives its philosophy from South Korean culture, particularly the balance between reason and feelings symbolized by *Tae Kuk*, the yin-yang symbol from the South Korean flag. In practice, the company begins product design by defining the geometric and technological elements (what it calls "reason"). After these specifications are defined, teams then enhance designs to inspire an emotional connection with the user ("feeling").

- **Methodology:** Samsung achieves its goals by thinking broadly—not just geographically, but also in terms of discipline. The company's staff of 700 designers conduct research in standard elements, such as branding and color, but also in a general range of fields, such as lifestyle research, human factors, and creative business planning.

Samsung prides itself on its broad approach to satisfying customer needs while maintaining a core sense of balance. The company establishes general themes that give local centers the flexibility to accommodate local market needs. For instance, while a European might like the same cell phone as someone in the developing world, the user in the emerging market might need a longer-lasting battery because of less frequent access to electricity.

Apple: Simplicity Is Not the Opposite of Sophistication

Apple is well known as one of the most innovative companies in the world, transforming many industries with the original Macintosh computer, iPod, iPhone, iPad, and other products. Here is the way the company executes creativity so consistently:[4]

- **Philosophy:** Steve Jobs has said, "Design is not just what it looks like and feels like. Design is how it works." The company's philosophy begins with building a deep understanding of a product's underlying principles. Apple seeks to marry simplicity and sophistication, driving the company to a relentless search for streamlining the physical package as well as the functionality.
- **Methodology:** Streamlining characterizes the design process as well, with development teams aware that they are creating not simply a product line, but an architecture that will serve as a platform for future products, such as by using similar operating systems in computers and accessories. Extensive initial testing for the original product guarantees that future products already have lower risk and greater reliability.

Management realizes benefits from this approach along the entire design chain. Employees transfer existing knowledge to derivative products, accelerating the internal design cycle. In production, the platform design provides for efficient procurement of assemblies and components. Customers also benefit from the shorter learning curve associated with adopting new products, thus facilitating the company's expansion in the marketplace.

REPHRASING THE QUESTION

Sir Alexander Fleming made the remarkable discovery of penicillin thanks to a sharp eye after a minor accident in the laboratory. Of this process, he once said, "One often finds what one is not looking for." (The famed scientist also once answered questions about a cure for the common cold with "A good gulp of hot whisky at bedtime. It's not very scientific, but it helps.")

How can you find what you are not looking for? There is no substitute for pretending to be the customer and asking different questions. A number of transformative products appeared just this way.

Palm: Do PDAs Compete with Computers or Paper?

Personal digital assistants (PDAs) made a brief and forgettable appearance in the 1990s when Apple released its Newton pad. It did not successfully penetrate the marketplace because of (among other things) poor handwriting recognition and a sense that the device was inconvenient. Several years later, Jeff Hawkins of Palm Computing launched the Pilot; with functionality limited to a contact list, a calendar, and a to-do list, it became the fastest-selling computer product in history.[5] The Palm Pilot offered two important features: synchronization with a personal computer and simplified handwriting recognition through the Graffiti program.

How did Hawkins determine his desired feature set? Legend has it that he perfected his vision by carrying a wooden prototype in his pocket during the day, pulling it out to pretend to write notes. In the process, he learned that the product competed with paper, not with computers. This key insight motivated him to focus design on a handwriting recognition program to offer applications similar to what people do (or did) with paper.

3M: Surgery Without Surgical Drapes

Manufacturer 3M has led innovation for more than 100 years, making products as diverse as sandpaper, circuit boards, and the ubiquitous sticky notes. Several years ago, the company used its Lead User innovative process (described in the sidebar) to ask how it could offer better surgical drapes.[6]

The development team began by studying infections and infectious environments, learning that in developing countries the common practice of using cheap antibiotics was very effective, albeit against a limited set of organisms. The 3M team expanded its research effort in many directions, such as to veterinarians, who pointed out that hairy patients who don't bathe require cheap and easy solutions.

At this point, the team began to ask, "How can we cheaply prevent infection without antibiotics or surgical drapes?" Further research and workshops introduced the team to an even broader set of relevant professionals, such as Hollywood experts who understood how to apply skin coverings that were nonirritating and easily removable.

Eventually the team arrived at the question "What is the revolutionary, low-cost approach to infection control?" Team members developed three concepts to answer this challenge, each of which was increasingly "outside the box" and mirrors the progressive nature of the concept definition process:

1. An economy line of surgical drapes
2. A "skin doctor" consisting of layered antimicrobial substances and a system to vacuum up blood during surgery
3. An "armor" line of coated catheters and tubes to prevent infection

You can see that the list expands far past simple surgical drapes. Rephrasing the question generated three completely different types of products.

MINICASE

3M's Lead User Innovative Process

The 3M Lead User process partners internal development with the market of interest. The process elements are as follows:

- Align your product with corporate strategy by identifying markets of interest and the level of innovation desired by stakeholders.
- Accelerate internal research by identifying domain experts and determining key trends.
- Shape product ideas in partnership with lead users to develop implementation plans and determine potential profitability.
- Develop breakthroughs in workshops, then hone product concepts and pricing models.

Kaiser Permanente: Designing Experiences, Not Buildings

In 2003, the health care organization Kaiser Permanente developed a strategy for attracting more patients and cutting costs.[7] Planning to replace hundreds of offices and buildings with new ones, the company hired IDEO to inform their design.

IDEO's teams investigated the operations of the current buildings and came to surprising conclusions. They discovered that because check-in was difficult and waiting rooms were uncomfortable, patients and families were annoyed from the moment they entered the facility. Patients became increasingly uncomfortable because they were typically forced to leave a companion in the waiting room and enter the examination room alone, where they would wait for about 20 minutes. The buildings operated inefficiently simply because doctors and assistants were situated too far apart.

Rather than provide basic architectural guidance, IDEO recommended a series of operational improvements. The suggestions included providing more comfortable waiting rooms with better check-in procedures. The team also proposed increasing the size of examination rooms to hold more people and providing curtains for added privacy. Finally, IDEO advocated redesigning corridors so that staff members could meet and increase their efficiency.

Adam Nemer, Kaiser's medical operations services manager, showed the importance of rephrasing the question when he said that "IDEO showed us that we are designing human experiences, not buildings. Its recommendations do not require big capital expenditures."

We all design human experiences.

ENVIRONMENTAL STEWARDSHIP AND DESIGN

Many companies are no longer satisfied with a mission motivated only by profit and have adopted goals of environmental stewardship and sustainable operation. Businesses in industries with a higher potential for environmental impact may find that sustainability is a wise marketing ploy; other corporate cultures may simply choose to support this value.

This section describes two companies that tightly link design processes with a sensitivity to environmental impact. Each business has developed its own methodology to evaluate product design based on environmental effects of manufacturing and waste processes.

Herman Miller: Cradle-to-Cradle Design

For many years, Herman Miller has been a major supplier to the U.S. office furniture industry with a "triple-bottom-line" philosophy of financial, environmental, and social responsibility.[8] To achieve its environmental sustainability goals, the company adopted a so-called cradle-to-cradle (C2C) design vision, named for the idea that at the end of their useful life, components should not serve as waste but rather as raw materials for new processes. C2C design is based on two key principles: design for eco-effectiveness rather than eco-efficiency, and waste equals food.

The first principle, eco-effectiveness, motivates the design of improved processes not just to minimize waste (this is eco-efficiency), but also to prevent waste from appearing in the first place. Inspired by nature, the second key concept requires that by-products of the manufacturing process or products reaching the end of their usable life must be either recyclable or biodegradable.

With C2C design as the underlying philosophy, Herman Miller uses its Design for Environment (DfE) process for implementation, which focuses on creating processes that prevent rather than minimize waste. The DfE product design methodology consists of four stages:

1. **Exploration:** The team broadly defines the product concept and specifications.
2. **Development:** The group divides the product into modules, assessing each for C2C compatibility in chemistry, disassembly, and recyclability, then analyzing tooling designs, product line designs, and ease of assembly.
3. **Launch:** The team focuses on finalizing the product and ramping up production.
4. **Maintenance:** Postlaunch, the company continues to assess the long-term impact and considers improved materials for later versions of the product.

Although this environmental review process requires extra evaluations, Herman Miller has built a corporate culture around it. As a result, the company also successfully leverages environmental sustainability in its marketing to both customers and prospective employees.

Patagonia: Everything We Make Pollutes

Patagonia has long been a world-renowned leader in outdoor clothing and products, known for high quality and innovative design.[9] Patagonia focuses its sales efforts on core users who simply enjoy athletic endeavors rather than those who might use the products for competition. Management attributes the ability to command higher price points for Patagonia products (as much as 20 percent higher than those of competitors) to both design and technical innovations.

Patagonia's mission statement states that the company will "build the best product, cause no unnecessary harm, and use business to inspire and implement solutions to the environmental crisis."[10] Product developers meet the stringent design objectives in two ways: they receive insight from "ambassadors," consultants who are leaders at their performance peak in various sports; and they have a field testing budget about twice that of Patagonia's competitors.

The company meets high quality standards by collaborating directly with fiber and fabric manufacturers to procure superior materials. Unlike its competitors, who outsource about 90 percent of their manufacturing to the developing world, Patagonia retains half its production capacity in North America and Europe, making it less of a perceived "sweatshop" operation. Management further conducts exhaustive research on the environmental effects of its manufacturing operations and works directly with suppliers to find substitutes for problematic raw materials, such as the use of organic cotton to minimize pesticide use.

Patagonia's operation is thus consistent with its marketing to nature lovers. Although the company does not have a single catchphrase for its philosophy, it has been widely recognized for its approach to quality design and global stewardship.

DESIGN AND BUSINESS BUILDING BLOCKS

While design interacts with all of a company's strategic functions, it is most closely linked with marketing. Design embodies the company's understanding of a product's value to the customer and thus captures the value proposition. To support a proprietary marketplace position, it is critical to create defensible intellectual property and fund a design effort consistent with your company's strategy. Furthermore, the product design strongly impacts manufacturing costs. Let's look at some of these links in detail.

Strategy

Your strategy will determine the importance of developing in-house capabilities for each stage of the product track. If your plan calls for advertising a strong and distinctive design method, hire top firms or a stable of creative professionals. Other competitive approaches may require less attention to design and more to later steps in the product track. This is closely linked to outsourcing decisions for manufacturers (discussed fully in Chapter 10).

Marketing

As explained in Chapter 4, you should determine how your design elements provide value to your target market. Remember Gillette's disposable blade design: later versions made it impossible to attach the blade upside down, presumably a clear improvement for people with early-morning vision issues.

Of course, a product generates sales only if you communicate the value clearly. Create a design whose features provide real benefits to users and quantify the value. A favorable (to you) pricing scheme should follow.

Intellectual Property

Design touches on many elements of intellectual property, including both the patent underlying the product's capabilities and any ornamental design features. Design includes all aspects of meeting the customer's needs, from fundamental applications to packaging.

Recall from Chapter 5 on intellectual property that when Gillette's team developed the Sensor razor, they patented seven designs but selected the one that was hardest to circumvent. Use intellectual property to strengthen your competitive position by using designs that are hard to bypass but provide the most value to customers.

Funding

Funding design is money well spent and is typically much cheaper than the remaining parts of the product development process. For highly differentiated products—that is, products that are not commodities—the design is often an integral part of the value proposition. Thus, you should plan to fund a design effort from the beginning rather than procrastinating. An important milestone in design is "design freeze," the point at which the final specifications are defined and the design is passed to the manufacturing group for implementation.

Eric P. Rose, NPDP, consultant and adjunct professor of product innovation at Pepperdine University, points out that at least 70 percent of the product's cost is determined by design freeze, and later manufacturing improvements can do little to improve the cost structure. Therefore, close interaction between design and manufacturing is critical to minimizing scheduling delays and development costs.

HINT

Design and Fundamental Business Elements

Determine first how your product impacts and improves the value you offer the customer, then evaluate whether your strategy calls for building strong design capabilities in-house or outsourcing them. This will also drive your intellectual property activities: will you share ownership with key manufacturers? Design teams must work in concert with manufacturing experts to minimize the cost of delays, particularly because the majority of the cost has been decided on by the time the design is finalized.

HINT

Design and Service Providers

As Adam Nemer, Kaiser's operations manager said, "We're designing human experiences, not buildings." Service providers should also consider design elements in developing new offerings. Format reports for maximum convenience to the reader. Always provide an overview or table of contents to demonstrate your sense of form and function. You can also combine your social and civic interests with your business, just as Patagonia highlights nature appreciation both in its philanthropy and sales efforts.

KEYS TO SUCCESS

Design has many roles in your business, reflecting and advertising your sensibilities and priorities. The process includes analyzing a product's required specifications, prioritizing its functions, and integrating them into a physical package. Design-oriented companies articulate clear philosophies based in disciplines ranging from engineering concepts to cultural influences. Methodologies typically call for multidisciplinary teams to combine their expertise, providing novel insights on customer needs. The design process can also include a response to environmental responsibilities; companies taking this route must closely integrate design with manufacturing to improve potential sources of waste or contamination.

Obtain a better appreciation of your customers' needs by putting yourself in their shoes; this often leads to unexpected insights on competitive substitute products and new ways to use your product. Your approach to product design needs to accurately reflect your company's strategy in terms of building long-term value.

Design doesn't just serve to advertise your product's capabilities; it also informs and demonstrates your corporate culture. In many ways, design is the last advertisement your customer receives prior to interacting with your product.

In *A Manual for Living*, the Greek philosopher Epictetus summed up the design process without realizing it (or maybe he did) in this statement: "No great thing is created suddenly, any more than a bunch of grapes or a fig. If you tell me that you desire a fig, I answer you that there must be time. Let it first blossom, then bear fruit, then ripen." Figs don't grow any faster today than they did in ancient Greece. Design is a long process of letting excellent teams bring creative ideas to maturity.

Chapter Quiz

1. *Rephrasing the question* refers to everything except which of the following?
   a. Expanding the intended market
   b. Identifying new competition
   c. Creating new product concepts for a target market
   d. Examining the competition's intellectual property
2. Product design includes everything except which of the following?
   a. Analyzing the required specifications
   b. Prioritizing the product's functional elements
   c. Reviewing the company's product road map
   d. Integrating functional elements into a physical package
3. Which of the following is *not* a component of the product trajectory?
   a. Design
   b. Human resources
   c. Integration
   d. Delivery
4. *Triple bottom line* refers to _____.
   a. financial, environmental, and social responsibility
   b. financial, strategic, and social responsibility
   c. environmental, financial, and legal responsibility
   d. social, customer, and strategic responsibility
5. Which intellectual property relationship is incorrect?
   a. The OEM retains IP ownership when a contract firm is used.
   b. The OEM shares IP ownership with a CDM.
   c. The ODM retains IP ownership.
   d. Only CDMs can have IP ownership.
6. What are the two key elements of design?
   a. Philosophy and methodology
   b. Strategy and intellectual property
   c. Philosophy and intellectual property
   d. Philosophy and marketing
7. Which of the following is *not* a stage in 3M's methodology?
   a. Alignment with corporate strategy
   b. Acceleration of internal research with external expertise
   c. Identification of competitors' ideas
   d. Development of breakthroughs in workshops

8. Design does *not* include which of the following?
   a. Competitors' philosophy
   b. Ornamental design
   c. Packaging
   d. Fundamental applications

9. What of the following is *not* a strategic consideration for design?
   a. The role of outsourcing in the company's approach to the product trajectory
   b. The fraction of the total cost set by design freeze
   c. The role of manufacturing in minimizing schedule delays
   d. The inability to change the company's strategy

10. Which of the following statements is *not* true?
    a. Design is intimately related to the value proposition.
    b. Design should remain separate from manufacturing to motivate the creative team.
    c. Design is the first phase of the product trajectory.
    d. Design reflects the company's sensibilities.

10

FABRICATION, INTEGRATION, AND DELIVERY

Risk comes from not knowing what you're doing.
—WARREN BUFFETT

As the marketing information in Chapters 3 and 4 may guide you in thinking about demand, this chapter should help you with supply. (It's interesting how we worry about demand first and supply later, but thinking about it in reverse would probably drive us out of business.) Traditionally, strategists group these activities under the heading of "manufacturing and distribution," but this chapter uses "fabrication, integration, and delivery" (FID) so as to include software.

FID choices extend far past simple material selection and packaging; they refer back to your underlying strategy. Do you license your technology or build the product yourself? Do you outsource the software development? All these decisions impact how you grow your business, particularly with respect to cash management.

You met Professor Eric P. Rose, an expert in product design and manufacturing, in Chapter 9. He explains that you must include manufacturing early in the strategic process to identify likely problems before "design freeze," when the team converges on a product's design and specifications and passes the product to the manufacturing group. Product development teams often struggle in compromising design elements with manufacturing realities.

If design and manufacturing must interact closely, why give design its own chapter separate from the rest of the product track? Because design has lower capital costs. Often product development proceeds in a stealthy manner through the design process, which is possible with limited investment in prototypes; however, scaling development to mass fabrication typically incurs major expenses in manufacturing companies. The high cash requirements of scaling product development to mass production mean that small risk factors can have enormous consequences.

Many factories successfully combine an outsourcing strategy with "lean," or just-in-time, approaches to minimize waste and optimize inventory levels. These methods work best with systems that report demand in real time, automatically stop machines if problems occur, and create environments in which everyone can contribute to steady improvement. Modern businesses have developed a number of new, creative solutions for both maintaining all the functions in-house and partnering with others in product manufacturing processes.

Software companies may not have the same capital requirements, but they do go through a similar process, integrating functional elements into larger packages. Software fabrication uses developers and servers instead of line management and capital equipment, but the product track still exists and is sensitive to the dynamics of outsourcing and cash management.

CONCEPT

Fabrication, Integration, and Delivery

The term *fabrication, integration, and delivery* refers to everything between the product design and its arrival in the customer's hands. It includes aspects of high-level decisions, such as the business model, and key implementation issues, such as material selection.

VERTICALLY INTEGRATED COMPANIES

Now we move to the nuts and bolts (literally) of FID. Companies are vertically integrated if they perform every element of the product track in-house and control the entire value chain, taking in raw materials and delivering finished products to customers.

We'll look at two such companies: Toyota and clothing manufacturer Zara. Both demonstrate similar approaches, even though one sells items for $20,000, and the other for $20.

CONCEPT

Vertically Integrated Companies
Vertically integrated companies perform every element of the product track in-house and control the entire value chain, taking in raw materials and delivering finished products to customers.

Toyota: Eliminating "Hurry Up and Wait"

For 30 years, the Toyota Way pioneered quality manufacturing processes; only with recent problems did the company face new scrutiny. Brake pedals notwithstanding, anyone interested in manufacturing should learn about the Toyota Way, which comprises the following elements:

- **Philosophy of lean manufacturing:** The Toyota Production System (TPS) minimizes waste through just-in-time, or lean, manufacturing. This system views each process as a customer of the preceding step, waiting for demonstrated demand prior to providing more parts. Thus, each step generates only the needed quantities. Lean manufacturing has grown in popularity because it reduces inventory across the entire supply chain and frees up cash.
- **Kanban:** Kanban systems visually indicate demand in a manufacturing facility to minimize excesses in production activity and inventory. A kanban sign originated as an actual card indicating that a bin or process was empty and needed more input. Today, electronic kanban systems use bar codes to transmit information directly into supply management databases.
- **Jidoka:** Toyota translates this term as "automation with a human touch." Jidoka systems are "smart" and signal problems by stopping auto-

matically and visually indicating when they cannot operate properly. This prevents the propagation of defective products throughout the system because the machine stops before it makes faulty parts. The automation allows one person to supervise many machines, enhancing productivity by requiring fewer people.

• **Kaizen:** Kaizen approaches call for employees at all levels to look at every process as a candidate for improvement; small upgrades compounded over time accumulate to achieve enormous advances. For this methodology to work, every employee must seek opportunities for refinement; effective kaizen requires a culture that empowers everyone to make suggestions.

CONCEPT

Lean Manufacturing

Lean, or *just-in-time*, *manufacturing* approaches consider each process to be the customer of the preceding one, allowing the company to manage inventory more tightly. This method works best with kanban systems that visually indicate when a process needs more input. Problems are addressed in real-time via jidoka systems that stop automatically when a problem arises, minimizing the flow of defective parts through the system. A culture of kaizen ensures continuous improvement at all levels of the organization.

Zara: "Five Fingers Touching the Factory and Five Touching the Customer"

New products from Spanish clothing manufacturer Zara go from design to shelf in only two weeks. Its rapid turnaround time and inventory management are the envy of the industry, leaving the company with unsold inventory accounting for less than 10 percent of stock (compared to the industry average of 17–20 percent).[1] The company's remarkable performance stems from its product development strategy and the methods it uses to accelerate inventory movement. Some of the key elements of Zara's systems include:

• **Philosophy:** After an early brush with near-failure, founder Amancio Ortega decided that "you need to have five fingers touching the factory and five touching the customer." He created Zara to be vertically integrated; that is, it would control the entire product track. In addition, the company has a relatively flat, horizontal organization to facilitate communication.

- **Information technology:** Zara constantly conducts market research, using customized handheld computers to connect retail stores with headquarters and sending hard data such as orders and sales trends, as well as soft data such as customer reactions. As corporate staff members receive this information, they can initiate the design process.

- **Manufacturing readiness:** Designers share work space with production planners and market specialists, facilitating rapid decision making. When the team is ready, designers transmit the specifications directly to the relevant cutting machines. The company uses elements of the Toyota Production System to manage the work process, such as bar codes that track pieces through the highly automated factories.

- **Contingency planning:** Management's overriding concern is to accelerate product delivery. Because tight capacity leads to increased wait times when demand increases, Zara's strategy calls for slight underutilization of its equipment to be ready for unexpected spikes. Similarly, the company purchases more than half of its fabrics undyed, so they are ready to be dyed at the last minute based on current trends in popular colors.

Zara's innovations comprise not just cool clothing, but also the information architecture that provides real-time trend data and kanban assembly systems for clothing. Even in the recession, the company generated a 5 percent increase in sales between 2008 and 2009. We should all be so lucky.

OUTSOURCING: DIVVYING UP THE PRODUCT TRACK

Whether you are a manufacturer, a software company, or a service provider, viewing the final product as an assembled series of components may motivate you to find others who can help with some of the processes. Outsourcing is the process of contracting with other companies to provide processes that are of lower value to your company. What looks like an unprofitable necessary evil to you may appeal to a company that profitably executes these functions. This is exactly why much of the American manufacturing, software development, and customer service industries migrated abroad.

CONCEPT

Outsourcing
Outsourcing is the process of contracting with other companies to provide processes that are of lower value to your company.

Global Trends

Toyota and Zara are vertically integrated, but they are in the minority today. Even small start-ups effectively contract with manufacturers in Asia. Why? What are the key drivers, and how did this shift happen? Contemporary product trajectories have been strongly affected by rapid and inexpensive distribution of information, goods, people, and capital:

• **Information:** By delivering information in real time, the Internet and cell phones have accelerated transparent processes within organizations and removed the seller-buyer information asymmetries in many fields. The information revolution has also transformed markets in digital products that have created new economies of scale (read *The Long Tail: Why the Future of Business Is Selling Less of More* by Chris Anderson for a terrific discussion of the consequences).

• **Goods:** Goods rapidly cross oceans and national borders; policy decisions in many countries to remove tariffs and other barriers have precipitated these moves. The capability to move goods cheaply and easily has transformed business around the globe. (It has also created interesting socioeconomic consequences throughout the world as capital flows to where it is most efficiently deployed.)

• **People:** People move freely to where capital and opportunities can be found; witness the collapse of Detroit, a city that depended entirely on the success of the American auto industry. By 2003, Detroit's population had declined to almost half its peak of 1.7 million people in 1960 to 900,000[2] as people migrated away from the urban center of the manufacturing industry. In fact, the recent financial crisis has served only as a coda to the lengthy decline of the heart of the city. Every day, ambitious people around the world have more liberty to seek productive employment (though this is sadly not an absolute truth everywhere); unfortunately for many American workers, this has led to a dramatic movement of jobs to other countries with determined workers and lower standards of living that offer decreased cost structures to employers. Although this means that competition is more fierce than ever, the flip side is that you are not geographically limited in finding business partners.

- **Capital:** It is easier than ever to find places to deploy capital efficiently. (The existence of good opportunities that provide a satisfactory return is another matter.) Trading in international public stocks is routine today, and improved communications facilitate international private investment. The only exception is start-ups that need heavy amounts of supervision, thus motivating local investment where experienced advisors can mentor the companies that receive their investments. This efficient capital movement means that opportunities must be of even higher quality to compete.

Cisco: OEM

How does management of an original equipment manufacturer (OEM) think? To understand the perspective of a company that outsources much of its manufacturing, let's look at Cisco, a company we're familiar with from Chapter 8. We have already seen that its acquisition process includes swapping employees with the target and that the company expedites product development with extensive use of milestones to measure the commitment of different groups. In recent years, it has accelerated its New Product Introduction (NPI) cycle, bringing more than 250 new products to market in 2008 alone.[3] Furthermore, as of early 2010, Cisco had more than 63,000 employees in 165 countries,[4] with almost half of the company's sales coming from outside the United States and Canada. Cisco is on the cutting edge of global operations.

To operate as an efficient global OEM, Cisco has a base of only four contract manufacturers, allowing it to work closely with them and leverage economies of scale without having to develop the capabilities in-house. The contract manufacturers were selected from an original set of 13 companies because of their design capabilities, capacity to build in large quantities, and ability to support many Cisco products. Suppliers have undergone a similar weeding process.

Cisco also uses its proprietary Autotest information system to show real-time data from its contract facilities for planning and quality control purposes, in essence, obtaining current data from someone else's factory. This allows management to use lean techniques even as it outsources much of its manufacturing.

Solectron: Contract Manufacturer

Solectron has grown into a global systems integrator by expanding its core competencies from simple manufacturing to general procurement, assembly, and logistics.[5] The company has thrived because of its smart strategic acquisitions and its relentless focus on customer service. It exemplifies a mind-set of studying its customers' customers to understand the broader marketplace.

The company manages most of the later functions in the product track, including all parts procurement, testing, service, and technical support, and it even participates in product design. This allows the OEM customer to focus on market research and product definition early in the process and later on sales and marketing.

Solectron's corporate culture has maintained an intense focus on quality and customer service, which is implemented through its weekly meetings covering internal customer satisfaction (Tuesdays), process and quality (Wednesdays), and customer satisfaction (Thursdays). This rigorous schedule paid off handsomely when Solectron became the first repeat winner of the prestigious Malcolm Baldrige National Quality Award.

As Solectron has grown, its competitive advantage has been transformed from manufacturing expertise to international logistics, which became more valuable as global trade continued to accelerate. Even though the company thus remained a contract design and manufacturing (CDM) firm in the OEM-CDM contract design scheme already described, Solectron provides additional value by leveraging its capabilities in "moving things internationally" as well as "making things internationally."

Putting It All Together

Because of the flow of information, goods, and people, both OEMs and contract manufacturers can exercise creativity in their approach to allocating phases in the product track. OEMs focused on design can still use modern lean techniques and other control systems to manage inventory levels. Meanwhile, contract manufacturers can keep an eye on the market by thoroughly understanding their customers' clientele. In short, companies that are not vertically integrated are more likely to succeed if they still have a thorough understanding of the other spokes in the wheel.

SOFTWARE: "THE INTERNET RUINED MY BUSINESS"

Consider software that we use every day: Microsoft Word, Apple Mail, Blackberry synchronization software—the list goes on. While these tools make us personally more productive (hopefully), they have virtually eliminated an entire cadre of functionaries. In other words, most software actually replaces people, beginning with clerks and assistants; today, sophisticated software even replaces higher-level people.

In addition, the global flow of information has destroyed more businesses than we can count. My friend served as an outsourced law librarian for many years, researching databases for lawyers; recently she told me, "The Internet ruined my business." Everyone now has access to data sources that were previously difficult to find. (As part of the wave of "creative destruction," a new crop of consultants has appeared; they conduct market research at home in their bunny slippers.)

MINICASE

Before Travelocity There Was SABRE

According to the SABRE website, a chance meeting on a 1953 flight triggered the modern era of automated seat assignments for the travel industry; a senior sales manager for IBM struck up a conversation with the president of American Airlines, discussing the handwritten logs used to keep seat reservations. Six years later, American Airlines and IBM announced plans to jointly develop the Semi-Automated Business Research Environment (SABRE), which went on to become the first real-time business application. (Unfortunately, it immediately led to a wave of associated staff reductions of approximately 30 percent.)

Software companies thus offer different value propositions and require new pricing models. To understand this better, let's look at product fabrication through the eyes of LegalZoom, which has mastered customized cookie cutters. Next are new models for integration via the music revolution led by Apple, which coupled hardware and software sales with new digital distribution. Finally, we'll look at Intuit's multiple distribution channels to see how this affects and creates new customer relationships.

LegalZoom: Designer Cookie Cutters

Today's customers can purchase many services on a Software-as-a-Service (SaaS) model, in which they need not install the application on their own computers. Instead, they access the software via the Internet and purchase it on a fee-for-service or an ongoing subscription basis. (A subscription model nicely follows the razor blade format we discussed in Chapter 4; it produces a high margin for recurring purchases because after the initial sale, marketing and distribution costs are extremely low.)

CONCEPT

Software-as-a-Service

Software-as-a-Service (SaaS) describes a model for software distribution where the user needs only Internet access to purchase the software on a subscription or fee-for-use basis.

LegalZoom is a good example of how to develop a fee-for-service model to generate customized products from a simple boilerplate. The application creates a questionnaire for the user, who can choose whether or not to purchase the output document afterward.

This has transformed the legal industry, because high hourly fees have long irritated consumers and businesses alike, particularly for routine needs. However, good lawyers know they can still charge handsome hourly rates for the time needed to review these simple documents. Mediocre lawyers should probably feel more threatened by this new way of buying straightforward agreements and forms.

Apple: Integrating Hardware and Software Products

We forget now that in the 1990s we listened to compact discs, and a six-disc changer was considered extremely advanced. This changed with the rapid rise of Internet access and the slow response of the record industry, which inspired a rash of illegal peer-to-peer sharing of digital music files. Record companies tried to develop their own online platforms but didn't want to share the technology with each other; consequently, digital piracy ran wild.

Into the vacuum stepped Apple, which sought to create an online experience that resembled buying music at a record store.[6] In 2001, Apple introduced the iPod digital music player, and in 2003, the iTunes Store followed, offering music downloads for $0.99 per song. The iTunes interface application manages audio and video files on a personal computer, taking standard know-how from the computer industry and turning the traditional music business upside down. Although it wasn't the first legal download site, Apple's domination of the music industry grew so much that by 2008, it led the United States in sales of digital music.[7] Twenty years ago, IBM never competed with record stores. Who knew this could happen?

Because Apple effectively serves as a music broker by licensing content from the large record companies, the digital rights management system must be airtight; in fact, it is managed as a trade secret rather than a patented algorithm. The $0.99 pricing is high enough to pay a royalty fee to the studio while still maintaining a healthy profit for digital products that have no inventory costs.

Of course, higher profits come from sales of iPod players and personal computers that integrate with the iTunes/iPod systems. Apple mastered a creative approach to hardware and software integration, reinventing the music industry along the way.

Intuit: Multiple Distribution Channels

Intuit made many accountants unhappy when it developed products like TurboTax, Quicken, and QuickBooks, allowing millions of people and businesses to manage their own finances at remarkably low prices. The company has created a strong brand, with loyalty reinforced by the sense that changing finance software packages introduces major headaches[8] (to say the least).

Intuit distributes its products through a number of channels. In retail stores like Staples and OfficeMax, strong brand equity gives Intuit products good shelf placement; these retailers also offer software through their online stores. In addition, Intuit sells its products through its own website, maintaining a direct line to customers without having to go through retailers. So some TurboTax buyers are actually customers of Staples or OfficeMax stores; some may be customers of Staples.com; and yet another set goes directly to Intuit's website. This creates marketing challenges in understanding how each of these customer segments chooses to reach Intuit and how the segments differ.

Intuit has expanded beyond simple software sales, creating a razor blade model by offering Web-based versions of core applications in addition to traditional downloads. This provides value to companies that desire multiuser access without investing in server maintenance and also simplifies the software upgrade and maintenance process.

In addition, Intuit offers add-on services like online bill paying, credit card processing, and payroll management; other less obvious add-ons that still provide additional value to businesses include services like website hosting, business card printing, and data backup services. Maybe Intuit will replace all your office staff: your accountant, your printer, your webmaster, and so on. . . .

FID AND BUSINESS BUILDING BLOCKS

When people speak about the difficulties of "execution," they usually refer to all the functions discussed in this chapter, when strategic planning is translated into action. While these activities support the company's strategy and marketing plan, manufacturing the product typically has the strongest impact in the funding arena as the company scales up production. As the company begins to commit significant resources, the risk factor escalates. Here, we will study how the FID activities reflect all the strategic elements.

Strategy

Decisions regarding FID are closely intertwined with corporate strategy and global economic trends. As you learned earlier, the explosive growth of consumer electronics in the 1970s forced the industry to split into marketing and manufacturing functions and drove many businesses to overseas factories. Companies faced the choice of managing far-flung empires to maintain cost-effective manufacturing or concentrating on customer relationships and letting others deal with the manufacturing functions. Today, businesses may seek out Chinese factories or Indian software developers in an attempt to reduce their costs; it is not clear that this always reduces risk. Consider Mattel's situation when they had to recall over a million Chinese-manufactured toys covered with lead paint in 2007. Presumably someone thought twice about the risk of foreign manufacturing after that affair.

In entrepreneurial ventures, management must decide how much manufacturing know-how to develop. Once the exclusive realm of large corporations, obtaining favorable contract manufacturing relationships is now easier than ever for start-ups. On the other hand, this can make technology licensing strategies even more attractive if manufacturing know-how does not present a strong barrier to entry.

Marketing

As we learned in Chapter 3, one of the classic marketing mix Four Ps is place, which describes logistics and distribution. Creating value far from the end users generates new challenges in delivering and servicing finished products, but companies in advanced countries find it difficult to obtain competitive labor rates locally.

One important trend is that small and large companies alike are on an equal footing to build relationships directly with customers if they can drive traffic to their websites. Simple tools like newsletters and promotions enable everyone to reach prospects directly. However, in today's world of abundant information, it is even more critical to hone your value proposition and communicate it effectively.

Intellectual Property

Intellectual property management represents a key component of any major strategic decision. As discussed in Chapter 9, the complex relationships available with contract design or manufacturing firms offer varying levels of proprietary protection. You need to decide where your real value originates; for instance, licensing your product concept to a firm that can take it to large-scale production more easily may bring you higher returns in a shorter time frame. Licensing is an easy way to bypass FID expenses, although the returns on development may be lower as a result.

Funding

FID decisions affect finance most of all. To see this, you need to understand the cash conversion cycle and working capital:

- **Cash conversion cycle:** The cash conversion cycle in Figure 10-1 illustrates how cash goes out to your vendors before it comes in from your customers. This cycle shows that you need to pay for the line workers and the raw materials before you make the item; then you have to market it before you sell it.
- **Working capital:** Defined in accounting as the difference between your current assets and your current liabilities, working capital is a key, intuitive driver of your business. Figure 10-2 shows that FID functions tie up substantial cash before customers can purchase your product.

Contract manufacturers have an advantage because they get paid on delivery to the OEM, not to the final customer. On the other hand, OEMs may be able to command higher margins because they sell directly to the customer, although they also have higher marketing risks. Entrepreneurs should realize how working capital requirements differ strongly between OEMs, contract manufacturers, and vertically integrated companies.

Delivery can tie up cash as well, but this depends on the industry. If you are an eBay vendor, you can require that the customer pay a separate charge for shipping at the point of purchase; therefore you receive your cash before

Figure 10-1   The Cash Conversion Cycle

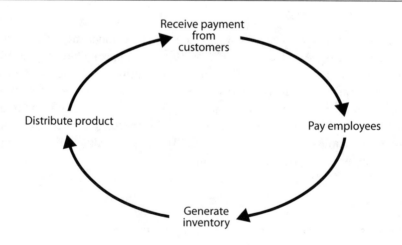

Figure 10-2   Cash Sinks in the Product Track

Design → Fabrication → Integration → Delivery

| Designers, prototypes | Personnel, inventory, quality control, contingency planning | Shipping services, warehousing |

you ship the product. On the other hand, driving a car off a dealer's lot means that the car must get from the factory to the dealer. Each industry has different standards for the effect of delivery on cash flow.

Creative solutions do exist; for instance, Zara's novel clothing manufacturing methods using kanban systems and other ideas borrowed from the auto industry. This operation actually requires negative working capital[9] because Zara sells its products just a few days after manufacturing, presumably before it needs to pay its vendors. This rapid cash inflow offsets the investment in extra production capacity.

HINT

FID and Fundamental Business Elements

If you decide to outsource, you must determine the implications for your intellectual property portfolio; however, your strategy may not call for developing all the resources and skill sets in-house. Most importantly, these activities tie up significant amounts of working capital, because in the cash conversion cycle, cash goes out to pay suppliers and vendors prior to receiving cash from a customer.

HINT

FID for Service Providers

Service providers don't face the capital investment requirements of manufacturers, but related issues exist. When work is outsourced to subcontractors or employees, agreements should clearly outline intellectual property ownership. Analyze the value of your product's different elements to determine which ones you can outsource. Large service providers of any kind—accounting, law, consulting—all use this model; junior people provide research, while senior members of the firm write high-level reports and handle direct interactions with customers. Number-crunching and analysis capabilities represent the fabricated "components," while the final legal opinion, consulting report, or audited financial statement is the service provider's "integration." Value is delivered through client relationships and presentations, typically the step with the highest margin for service providers.

In addition, outsourcing or hiring presents the same challenges with working capital; namely, that you will likely pay your vendor before you receive the customer's check. This generates its own set of needs for cash management.

KEYS TO SUCCESS

Fabrication, integration, and delivery represent the stages of the product track between product design and the customer's purchase. In a manufacturing environment, they involve managing inventory and designing processes that minimize waste and defects. Analysis of the most profitable FID approach requires a fundamental understanding of how you provide value to your customers and identification of the processes that may be outsourced without loss of quality. Even if you partner with other design or manufacturing firms, it is still possible to use technology to create a lean manufacturing environment.

Software companies have new opportunities in these functions, creating hybrid solutions such as customization, availability, or novel integration with hardware. Software-as-a-Service models allow companies to repackage their products so they are available in fee-for-service or subscription form, creating openings to provide customers with added value.

Decisions regarding your company's FID know-how are central to its strategy and affect its activities in various disciplines, such as marketing, design, and intellectual property management. However, this decision most strongly affects company finance because it defines working capital requirements.

At this point, we are about to leave the manufacturing environment and return to a marketing mind-set; as Charles Revson, founder of Revlon Cosmetics, once said, "In the factory we make cosmetics; in the drugstore we sell hope." In the next chapter, we will watch the transformation from cosmetics to hope.

Chapter Quiz

1. **What is another term to describe lean manufacturing?**
   a. Outsourced
   b. Just-in-time
   c. Vertically integrated
   d. Just-for-strategy
2. **Software often replaces _____ .**
   a. strategy
   b. capital goods
   c. people
   d. lean manufacturing
3. **Which of the following is *not* part of the product track?**
   a. Design
   b. Marketing
   c. Integration
   d. Fabrication
4. **Outsourcing is _____ .**
   a. illegal in some countries
   b. important to vertically integrated companies
   c. a contract process
   d. a required part of lean manufacturing
5. **Which of the following is *not* included in important global movement?**
   a. Information
   b. Goods
   c. People
   d. Strategy

6. *SaaS* refers to _____ .
   a. Software-as-a-Service
   b. Strategy-as-a-Strength
   c. Software-as-a-Strategy
   d. Software-as-a-Strength

7. Which of the following statements is *not* true about fabrication, integration, and delivery?
   a. They refer to everything after product design.
   b. They are not related to the marketing Four Ps (place).
   c. They include high-level decisions, such as outsourcing practice.
   d. They include implementation issues, such as material and vendor selection.

8. What is a key philosophy of lean manufacturing?
   a. Extra inventory must be kept in case of demand spikes.
   b. Outsourcing doesn't work.
   c. Design is not important.
   d. Every process is a customer of the preceding one.

9. CDM is an acronym for _____ .
   a. contract design manufacturer
   b. contract design marketing
   c. competing design manufacturer
   d. contract design measurement

10. Which Japanese term is *not* part of the Toyota Production System?
    a. Kanban (signs)
    b. Gijutsu (technology)
    c. Kaizen (improvement)
    d. Jidoka (automation)

11

LAUNCH

The aim of marketing is to make selling superfluous.
The aim of marketing is to know and understand the
customer so well that the product or service fits him
and sells itself.

—PETER DRUCKER

A t this stage, your product is almost ready! The assembly lines are humming along, and you're ready to announce your presence in the marketplace. Where do you start? How can you do this without sounding like the proverbial used car salesman?

Your overarching goal now is to instill confidence. You may know your product inside and out, but the customer still sees it as an unknown quantity. You're back to the role we defined in Chapter 1: management reduces risk. You must show the prospect that there is little or no risk associated with trying or switching to your product. Therefore you need to decide whom you are convincing and then reach out to this group with an effective marketing campaign.

This chapter starts with formal advertising theory and the key elements of a communications campaign. Next it looks at the characteristics of people who buy a new product. Who's likely to take on the risk associated with your product? How does the receiver of your communication change as your product matures?

We'll put this theory into practice with two types of situations that demand this kind of communication. First, we'll study two examples of successful product launches, examining how they apply the advertising basics effectively. Second, we will look at recalls, because they entail similar advertising challenges.

FIVE Ms OF ADVERTISING

In launch, you advise your prospect that your new product is available, it solves a problem, its value proposition exceeds anything else on the market, and the risk of failure is low. Obviously you are conveying quite a bit of information, and it can be hard to get your arms around that challenge. How do you create the right plan?

You have already learned about the marketing Four Ps; now we will cover the Five Ms of advertising: mission, message, medium, money, and measure. Let's look at each item:

- **Mission:** What is the campaign objective? Whom are you trying to reach? For instance, you may seek to branch out into another market segment or raise brand awareness in your existing market. Budweiser is legendary for its creative Super Bowl commercials, so its current mission may simply be to reinforce that fun-loving spirit.
- **Message:** What are you trying to say? You can create different messages for various targets, but be consistent in your approach. One insurance company drives me crazy, because sometimes its ads focus on cavemen and other times on gecko lizards; the commercials for one of its competitors show prices from different companies rolling down against a stark white background. Guess which one I understand?
- **Medium:** How do you reach your target? Ads for new books often appear in the *New York Review of Books* for obvious reasons. Medium selection encompasses everything from buying Super Bowl time to the paper quality for your brochures.

- **Money:** What is the budget for your advertising campaign? What kind of returns do you expect to generate? This varies strongly with industry. Bill Matthies, an expert in consumer electronics, likes to remind entrepreneurs that any budget under $20 million is considered tiny in that field. Generally, you can create an economical, reasoned campaign; however, there are some positioning problems that money can't solve (more on this later).
- **Measure:** How effective was your marketing? Google became a household name by answering this question. While click-through rates and other analytical tools make Internet marketing easy to analyze, you may need to estimate the usefulness of traditional marketing, such as attendance at your trade show booth or networking success.

CONCEPT

Five Ms of Advertising

The *Five Ms* of advertising are mission, message, medium, money, and measure.

INNOVATION DIFFUSION THEORY

In his classic *Diffusion of Innovations*, Everett Rogers described how technologies migrate through populations.[1] Basically, one person tries it, then another hears about it or sees it in action and follows suit; someone else sees it and follows again. In other words, innovation diffusion is actually a social process; at some point, it has less to do with the product and more to do with personalities, relationships, and communication. (Malcolm Gladwell beautifully captured the mechanics of these interactions in his book *The Tipping Point*.) Rogers popularized the diffusion curve shown in Figure 11-1.

Although Rogers called the first to sign on innovators, we will use the term *innovative adopters* to differentiate them from the innovators using this book. Innovative adopters are followed by early adopters, then the early and late majorities, and finally the laggards. Each group adopts the product for different reasons and is inspired by different social incentives.

Figure 11-1   Innovation Diffusion in a Population

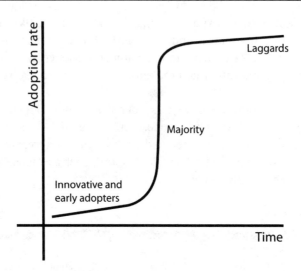

Innovation Diffusion

Innovation diffusion is primarily a social process that depends on both the product and social characteristics such as personalities, relationships, and communication.

This curve has profound implications. You can't sell to the entire population at first because everyone is simply not hardwired to buy a new product, but you do need to convince the innovative adopters. We all know people like this—your friend with the newest cell phone, the guy with the newest car. (Chapter 4 discussed the value proposition driving this type of person.) Therefore, your launch program must focus on convincing these group members that they need your product.

In other words, as the product goes through its life cycle, you must gear your marketing toward people with different risk tolerances, as shown in Figure 11-2. Innovative adopters naturally have an affinity for higher risk

Figure 11-2   Risk Affinity of the Target Market Throughout a Product
Life Cycle

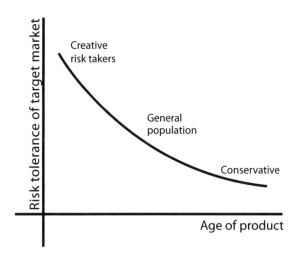

than do the laggards, who are generally more conservative. Thus, it is better to match your launch campaign to the innovative adopters who are willing to take on the risk of the new product. A mature product calls for a different type of communication campaign.

In his bestselling *Crossing the Chasm*, Geoffrey A. Moore discusses how the different risk profiles between the early adopters and the early majority creates a discontinuity because the new adopters excitedly take on a new technology . . . and then the process stalls out.[2] Moore explains that the early adopters are visionaries seeking breakthroughs, whereas the early majority is composed of pragmatists seeking improvement. Bridging this gap (the chasm of the title) is a fundamental challenge for innovators, because the product offers different benefits to each group. (Recall from Chapter 4 that value propositions motivate your customer to buy; for each of the groups identified by Moore, the value proposition is fundamentally different.)

Moore recommends that to bridge this gap, you must define and conquer a niche market and then extend your reach into mainstream markets. Below I will describe the importance of the segmentation-targeting-positioning approach, the classic method for disaggregating a broad market to find the elements best aligned with your product and company.

SOCIAL MEDIA

Social media, and reviews in particular, play an interesting role in today's advertising campaigns, because they act where the Five Ms meet the mechanics of innovation diffusion.

Customer reviews are effective because the mission appears so altruistic—namely, to inform fellow shoppers. The message can be displayed clearly with a five-star rating system and supplemented with comments as necessary. Because people use the Internet for research, the medium is particularly effective in finding those who have already shown interest. The cost of advertising is significantly cheaper than other mass media, and a pay-per-click scheme converts it into a variable cost. Finally, click-through measurement is straightforward.

The real beauty of social media, however, lies in the way it accelerates the diffusion process. Figure 11-1 shows diffusion taking place over an unspecified time period that is defined by how long it takes for innovative adopters to come in contact with members of their networks to demonstrate new technology. With social media, you can instantly reach out to your network.

Thus, social media is not new, merely faster. It integrates the innovative adopter's broadcast tendencies with the Internet's accessibility and measurement capabilities. It has the added benefit of reaching network members outside the innovative adopter's usual circle; that is, those members he or she doesn't see frequently. Thus the innovative adopter accesses his or her full network and influences everyone within a faster time frame.

LAUNCH

Launch is the process of announcing a new product's availability and satisfying the first customers. Thus, it poses a sales and communication challenge, because you educate the target market, as well as an operational challenge, because you must successfully deliver the product.

When you educate the target market, you are creating a niche for yourself in the prospect's mind. This activity is called positioning. As mentioned in earlier chapters, the classic *Positioning: The Battle for Your Mind* by Al Ries and Jack Trout details a number of marketing strategies and tactics. After a brief refresher on positioning, we will look at two cases of successful launches, highlighting the elements of the Five Ms that were used most effectively.

Positioning Revisited

We talked about positioning in Chapter 3 in conjunction with market segmentation and targeting; many problematic introductions are actually positioning mistakes. (Search the Internet for "failed product launches" when you need a good laugh. New Coke is just the beginning. Anyone interested in Bic underwear?) In such cases, companies who try to expand their brand usually don't understand their current position and thus can't leverage it.

By definition, a successful launch creates the position you seek. Both companies described here had a clear understanding of their desired positions and found multiple opportunities to reach their targets. Of course, these companies had significant budgets, so money may not have been as much of a factor as it is for your next project; however, big budgets often create their own disasters (as with New Coke and Bic underwear).

BMW: The Marketing Mix Is Shaken, Not Stirred

Remember yuppies? In the 1980s they ruled Wall Street and drove BMWs. However, in the 1990s BMW sought to move from its role as a German-made symbol of yuppie affluence to a global luxury brand offering the "ultimate driving machine."[3] Becoming a global brand was not just talk; the company's sweeping changes included opening its first factory in the United States. In addition, management put weight behind the luxury reputation by improving service offerings at its dealerships.

Corporate goals revolved around providing the world with best-in-class cars that held well-defined positions in the marketplace. This effort culminated in the launch of the BMW Z3 roadster. Market studies revealed that it appealed to people who saw themselves as "loving life" and sought to express their individuality through their cars. These prospects identified themselves by their attitude, not their demographic, making traditionally segmented advertising inappropriate. This adventurous mentality tracked well with the risk tolerance of innovative adopters, and the Z3 made an excellent flagship product to represent the new company image.

In 1995, BMW saw a major opportunity in MGM's upcoming release of the James Bond film *GoldenEye*. The charming, sexy, highly individual hero mirrored the self-image of BMW's prospects. MGM wanted to jump-start the James Bond franchise and began by hiring Pierce Brosnan to star in the movie. Seeking to enhance its own publicity campaign, the studio created a partnership with BMW. It was a natural fit since fast, fun, elegant cars like the Aston-Martin had always represented an important element of James Bond's image. This advertising partnership took product placement to a new level of sophistication because the car didn't just appear onscreen; it was worked into the movie's dialogue: "Now, pay attention Bond. First your new car. A BMW . . ."

Ultimately Bond wasn't the only one with a new BMW; when the automaker had booked nearly twice the number of forecast orders by the end of 1995, the comarketing was considered a success. Although the *GoldenEye* release took place in concert with other marketing activities, it certainly led the charge. MGM benefited as well when *GoldenEye* had the largest opening weekend in the studio's history, grossing more than $26 million in ticket sales.

The BMW case demonstrates how you can create exciting opportunities if you understand what really makes your prospect tick. Don't focus solely on how your prospects view you; think about how they view themselves and demonstrate how your product echoes that sentiment.

Lilly: A Prozac Education

Once upon a time, people were embarrassed to talk about depression or mental illness. Then we discovered Prozac.

In 1987, pharmaceutical company Eli Lilly and Company revolutionized psychiatric treatment by introducing selective serotonin reuptake inhibitors (SSRIs).[4] Previously, the company had focused on insulin, antibiotics, and vaccines; SSRIs represented a significant shift in its target diseases. More important, it represented a new approach to an old medical problem and thus required novel tactics.

Lilly began with a process similar to the 3M Lead User process discussed in Chapter 9. Team members worked closely with 150 leading psychiatrists in a mutual education process about the treatment of depression and the pharmacology of SSRIs. Many of these experts eventually spoke on behalf of the company at conferences, symposia, and meetings. Lilly's educational effort expanded to primary care physicians in hopes that they also would feel comfortable prescribing the medication. The key message to this group was that Prozac was simpler to administer than the previous generation of antidepressants because the dosage levels were less sensitive and required less tweaking.

To the FDA, Lilly promoted messages regarding the efficacy of SSRIs and the long-term safety. Similar information went to drug formulary committees at hospitals and managed care organizations, whose interest lay in the opportunity to reduce expenses associated with hospitalization and counseling. Ultimately, the company's campaign consisted of a number of messages that were fine-tuned to each audience; these messages represented different angles on Prozac's benefits.

The central key to Prozac's success lies in the company's redefinition of depression as a biochemical disorder instead of a behavioral choice. Leaders didn't just reposition the product or even the company, *they repositioned the problem.* Lilly's approach transformed an entire culture that stigmatized mental illness into one that focused on medication and treatment.

The hidden nature of depression brought an interesting side effect (so to speak). Because people had been ashamed to discuss their condition, Lilly's team simply didn't know the extent of the global antidepressant market, guessing that the size was less than $500 million and that annual revenues for the company could reach $70–100 million. How many people could possibly be depressed?

Well, a lot. Prozac set a new bar for blockbuster drugs, generating $3 billion annually for the four years that it didn't have competition. Ongoing clinical trials expanded the market to patients with bulimia, anxiety and panic disorders, premenstrual syndrome, and many other behavioral and mood disorders. The American antidepressant market grew from $400 million in 1986 to $8 billion by 2004 (and reached $17 billion worldwide). There is no question that Prozac changed psychiatry—and transformed Lilly as well.

RECALLS

As I write this, Johnson & Johnson (J&J) has just announced a recall of several children's cold remedies (talk about a touchy situation for retaining customer confidence!). Toyota is frantically recovering from damage done to its sterling reputation by faulty brake pedals. Imagine yourself in the Toyota chairman's office, listening to tape of a 911 call recorded moments before your brakes caused a fatal crash. Faulty products can obviously be devastating to everyone.

How do you restore confidence, especially in today's litigious environment where sympathy could imply liability? The principles of promoting education and clear messages apply to recalls just as they do to launches. An excellent *Harvard Business Review* article by N. Craig Smith, Robert J. Thomas, and John A. Quelch summarizes the key steps in restoring trust as follows:[5]

- **Take customers' concerns seriously.** No one likes to hear that their fears are unimportant.
- **Address the problem honestly and humbly.** Share your understanding of the situation, even when it's limited; this is not the time for an ostrich impersonation.
- **Make your customers whole via refunds or replacements.** Customers want to see generosity from companies, regardless of liability concerns.
- **Reintroduce your improved product.** Your recalled product represents your toughest competition; make the distinction clear.

I'll now introduce two cases of companies handling their recalls in vastly differently ways. Johnson & Johnson set the modern standard for crisis management after the infamous Tylenol poisonings. On the other hand, Intel demonstrated that arrogance can make a recall's costs skyrocket when a user's discovery of a flaw in the Pentium chip turned into a public relations disaster.

Tylenol: Turning Disaster into Action

In the fall of 1982, seven people in the Chicago area died mysteriously in the space of a few days. Two off-duty firemen monitoring their police radios noticed that Tylenol was mentioned in two reports and suggested that the over-the-counter drug could be involved. The rapid investigation that followed determined that Tylenol laced with cyanide had caused the deaths; in pills from bottles used by the victims, the red half of the capsule was swollen and discolored, and the pills had a telltale almond scent.[6] In the ensuing chaos, the Illinois attorney general suggested that "a disgruntled employee in the production chain" was the culprit. Advertising experts claimed that the brand would be gone in a year.

J&J swung into action by recalling 31 million bottles of Tylenol capsules and offering replacement tablets for free.[7] It also worked closely with authorities to accelerate the investigations. The company ultimately verified that it was a crazed individual who had bought the capsules, filled them, then returned them to the store; most important, it was not an employee. What could the company do to look responsible for the solution but not the problem?

Management addressed the disaster directly with an extensive public relations campaign.[8] Chairman James Burke appeared on the "Phil Donahue Show" and "60 Minutes" to address fears and explain that the poisonings were committed by a terrorist outside the organization, not inside the company.

Within two months, J&J announced that Tylenol capsules would be available again in new triple-sealed containers. This campaign was married to attractive pricing: the company widely inserted coupons in newspapers to motivate consumers to return. It also provided 25 percent discounts to retailers who would order the same volumes of Tylenol as they had before the scare. Advertising messages focused on restoring trust. Newspapers carried updates on the scare and the improved packaging, enhancing the extensive public relations campaign.

Ultimately, the entire episode cost the company around $100 million, but it paid off. With the announcement of the tamperproof containers, J&J's stock recovered almost fully; within a year, the company had regained most of its market share.

The public relations campaign would not have enjoyed success if it hadn't been aligned with the company's sense of responsibility to the community. The recall and new tamperproof packaging ensured that the poisonings would not recur. When Burke appeared as the company's face to assuage fears and demonstrate the actions he had taken, consumers were ready to hear his message and trust J&J again.

Pentium Bug: "Replacement Is Simply Unnecessary for Most People"

On October 30, 1994, Thomas Nicely, a mathematics professor at Lynchburg College, reported a flaw in the Pentium chip to Intel, as well as to several experts. With the Internet a newly emerging forum, word of the defect spread rapidly throughout the industry. Unfortunately, Intel remained quiet. In November, an article appeared in *Electronic Engineering Times*, a trade journal; the mainstream press found it and began to publish more information.

The story snowballed and created a public relations disaster, culminating in a *New York Times* article titled "Intel Facing a General Fear of Its Pentium Chip."[9] The author cited examples of scientists performing precision calculations for particle physics and military applications and finding problems. To make matters worse, jokes on the Internet proliferated ("At Intel, quality is job 0.99").

When IBM halted shipments of computers containing the chips, Intel promised to replace chips for those users the companies viewed as at risk. Who exactly fell into this category? The *New York Times* article cited Intel's claim that the average computer user would encounter the problem only once in 27,000 years of calculations, whereas IBM reported that the problem could appear once every 24 days. So who qualified for the recall? How was Intel going to address those at risk? Quoted in the *New York Times* article, Florida Deputy Attorney General Pete Antonacci captured the general mood when he said, "They've got to stop acting like a rinky-dink two-person operation in a garage and start acting like the major corporation they are."

The day after publication of the *New York Times* article, Intel announced its recall with a humbling statement from Andrew Grove, the CEO: "The past few weeks have been deeply troubling. What we view as an extremely minor technical problem has taken on a life of its own. . . . We are today announcing a no-questions-asked return policy on the current version of the Pentium processor. Our previous policy was to talk with users to determine whether their needs required replacement of the processor. To some people, this policy seemed arrogant and uncaring. We apologize. We were motivated by a belief that replacement is simply unnecessary for most people. We still feel that way, but we are changing our policy because we want there to be no doubt that we stand behind this product."[10]

While Intel has recovered 15 years later, the Pentium bug still looms as a classic case of bungled corporate public relations. Be honest, be generous, be sorry, fix the problem. It's really that simple.

LAUNCH AND BUSINESS BUILDING BLOCKS

Although *launch* sounds like the beginning, it really reflects the end of the product development process. At this point, your company has already implemented its strategy regarding resource management, organizational design, and outsourcing elements of the product track. A product launch's primary function is to execute the marketing plan, identifying and communicating to the prospects who are most likely to accept the risk (and perhaps gaining the added rush) of using a new product. Although launch is primarily concerned with marketing, it must be supported by an intellectual property and funding program. Let's look at some of the details.

Strategy

Who is your competition? What is your position today? Position is not just an advertising choice; it defines a major component of your strategy. Use your product launch to accelerate your company's motion toward its vision. BMW wanted to be a global luxury brand rather than a precision German tool, so it advertised that its hip new roadster was built in the United States and offered improved dealer service. Walk the walk.

Marketing

The marketing Four Ps are critical here: quality product, attractive pricing, creative advertising (promotion), convenient distribution (place). Articulate the distinction from your competition; in recalls, you differentiate your renewed product (or company) with the original. Think carefully about how your prospects view your product, not how you see it. Reach out to those people who see themselves as more risk tolerant; introduce your product to them and let them do your advertising for you.

Intellectual Property

By the time a product launches, it is typically too late for patent development. In fact, this is the time when the investment in intellectual property pays off, because now you can finally articulate the value, encompassed by the features that are provided by your proprietary competitive advantage. It is even easier to explain the added value if you can capture someone's attention with a clever advertising campaign or an eye-catching logo; this warrants further investment in intellectual property.

Funding

Consumer advertising campaigns are typically expensive compared to marketing to businesses (you don't generally advertise industrial gizmos on TV). When you plan your product development budget, estimate launch expenses generously. Hire good agencies that will execute your plan to make your product memorable. Execute the launch program in the quarter before you will be shipping the product so that people are primed but not bored by it. Finally, note how this affects your cash conversion cycle; cash goes out to advertising before it generates revenues.

HINT

Relationship of Launch to Fundamental Business Elements
Product launch is primarily a marketing and finance activity since you have already implemented much of your strategy. Your marketing program should focus on articulating your competitive advantage and preparing your customer

for the upcoming product availability. Leverage all of the Four Ps—product, price, place, and promotion—to heighten interest in your brand. The finance function is critical at this time, because these activities are expensive; without them, however, who even knows that your product exists?

HINT

Launches for Service Providers

Service providers face the same challenges of communicating in a noisy marketplace. Touch your prospects in novel ways and actively determine your position in the market. Like a manufacturer, you have access to cost-effective "buzz" generators and inexpensive customizable advertising, such as social media platforms and newsletters. Use them wisely so that you educate but don't overwhelm your customers. Unlike a manufacturer, you can provide value while you promote via educational programs, enhancing your credibility without irritating people.

KEYS TO SUCCESS

Launching a product involves educating your prospect regarding your product's availability. The Five Ms of advertising—mission, message, medium, money, and measure—form the building blocks of a focused marketing plan. This advertising campaign changes over time because your first customers, the innovative adopters, differ in personality from the vast majority of your future customers. Sell to the innovative adopters, and let them sell to everyone else.

Create advertising plans that approach your target market segment appropriately. Like BMW, you can show off your product in novel media, speaking directly to prospects and mirroring what they want to hear. The Prozac launch teaches us how to forge messages tuned directly to a specific target and how to position not just a product, but the underlying problem as well.

No one wants to face a recall, but they do happen. Businesses do not fail from demonstrating too much integrity. Be honest and fair, and make your customers whole. If you approach both launch and recalls with an attitude of fairness and a genuine interest in providing value, your company will thrive.

Now what? In the final chapter, we will learn how to wrap up a project, then spend some time covering trends that shape modern product development.

Chapter Quiz

1. Which of the following strategies is *not* recommended for recalls?
   a. Take customers' concerns seriously.
   b. Address the problem honestly and humbly.
   c. Articulate that you have no responsibility for the problem.
   d. Make your customers whole via refunds or replacements.
2. Innovation diffusion does *not* depend on which of the following?
   a. Intellectual property protection
   b. Group communication
   c. Product quality
   d. Adopter personality
3. In launch advertising, the *mission* refers to the _____.
   a. corporate values
   b. campaign's objective
   c. customer's needs
   d. company's advantage
4. Positioning means _____.
   a. developing an elaborate advertising campaign
   b. creating a niche for yourself or your product in the prospect's mind
   c. segmenting your prospects
   d. providing value
5. Which of the following does *not* describe launch?
   a. An operational challenge because you are delivering finished products
   b. A sales challenge because you must educate your target market
   c. A marketing challenge because you are positioning your product
   d. A strategic challenge because you are choosing your intellectual property
6. Why do launches and recalls present similar advertising problems?
   a. In launches you deliver product, and in recalls you take it away.
   b. Intellectual property protection must remain intact.
   c. Communication focuses on inspiring customer confidence and reducing risk.
   d. The product inception process is the same.

7. Communication enablers have a different adoption model because they
_____ .
   a. accelerate progress
   b. don't have innovative adopters
   c. cannot support advertising campaigns
   d. attain value only when more people have it

8. Who are the most risk-tolerant adopters?
   a. Majorities
   b. Innovative adopters
   c. Laggards
   d. Early adopters

9. Which is *not* one of the Five Ms of advertising?
   a. Marketing
   b. Medium
   c. Measure
   d. Mission

10. In launch advertising, what does the term *money* refer to?
   a. The advertising budget
   b. The product price
   c. The product cost
   d. The customer's budget

12

WRAP-UP

Where you start is not as important as where
you finish.

—ZIG ZIGLAR

Finished! It's hard to believe that we have taken a product from concept to strategy, through marketing analysis, and into the funding cycle. After delving deep into the sausage factory (and this applies to e-sausages as well), we returned to the world of marketing. Now we need to close the loop and determine how we can learn from this experience and make the next product even more successful.

This chapter describes the methods used by two companies for successful postmortems, or project wrap-ups. Many organizations don't consider a product complete until they have reflected on the process, giving everyone a chance to celebrate successes and uncovering problems so that mistakes are not repeated. The negative connotation stems from the origin of the term *postmortem*, meaning literally "after death" and describing examinations of dead bodies. Fortunately, project postmortems, though difficult, are not that bad—and they typically lead to real organizational change.

The second part of the chapter makes some observations regarding strategies for success in product development. They stem from my many years developing technologies, products, and businesses. As usual, I will borrow liberally from newspaper articles to uncover important trends and highlight common traps.

POSTMORTEMS

Like other rites of passage, postmortems serve many roles in product development because they bring closure to one phase and prepare everyone for the next. At NASA, they are referred to as "lessons learned" (probably to avoid the reference to dead bodies), but the principle echoes that of corporations: providing a vehicle so team members can effectively contribute their experiences to the corporate memory bank, capturing both successes and failures. Often companies publish an internal document that summarizes these lessons and is ideally reduced to a simple checklist for the next time a similar project begins. This is true for wedding planners and manufacturers alike.

CONCEPT

Postmortem Reviews

Postmortem reviews combine individual experiences into a corporate memory and bring closure to a project. In these sessions, the team reviews the entire project to highlight elements that worked well and determines areas for improvement.

Pixar: Admitting That People Don't Like Postmortems

The animation leader Pixar takes postmortems seriously.[1] Management starts with the assumption that although postmortems are good for the individual and the organization, people simply don't like them. First of all, no one enjoys revisiting the past when a project is finally over. In addition, leaders prefer to praise their good employees—and the employees want to be celebrated! Generating interest in an honest postmortem thus presents an extra challenge to management swimming upstream.

To optimize the outcome, Pixar has developed an effective postmortem process with simple techniques that include the following:

- **Vary the format:** Using the same structure will generate the same results, so vary how you host the meeting.
- **Create balance:** Ask the group to list five things they would do again, as well as five they wouldn't. This balance between positive and negative aspects creates a safer space to explore room for improvement.
- **Use quantifiable data:** Enter the room with hard facts, such as the time needed for specific processes or the number of times an element was reworked. This keeps the discussion from getting personal and allows the group to identify systemic problems.

Microsoft: Asking the Right Questions

If Microsoft has one management sweet spot, it is process, from project inception to postmortem review.[2] Once a project is completed, the team waits a few weeks (in my experience, to let them "sleep on it" and distill their observations) prior to setting up the postmortem meeting.

To maintain objectivity, the company turns to someone outside the project to manage the review in a half-day workshop. The facilitator organizes the meeting with an agenda that's distributed ahead of time and sticks to the schedule during the meeting. The venue is extremely important: everyone sits comfortably at a round table so there is no "boss." The organizer typically uses tools, such as colored markers and a flip chart, to organize points as they are made, enabling someone to take notes for an accurate summary afterward. The discussions are structured around questions such as these:

- How can we improve the planning process and getting the project off the ground?
- What were our biggest mistakes in scheduling?
- Which steps were project bottlenecks, and how can we improve them?
- Were the project requirements reasonable and well thought out?
- Was everyone's role on the team appropriate and communicated well?

Of course, each of these questions typically generates a waterfall of follow-up discussion, but that's the point. By creating the right environment, the right observations will emerge, and the organization as a whole can learn.

MINICASE

Microsoft Postmortem Environment

In a postmortem, maintaining a productive atmosphere is vital to prevent a meeting from degenerating into a blame game or mutiny. Microsoft creates this environment by suggesting a few key rules of conduct. Everyone must be

- **Self-critical:** People must check their egos at the door.
- **Professional:** Do not include references to personal issues.
- **Factual:** Do not offer opinions, but do bring data.
- **Brief:** Make the process efficient.

STRATEGIES FOR PRODUCT SUCCESS

We have now taken development from the earliest concept to the launched product. Along the way, we have tackled many of the strategic elements, such as identifying market opportunities and offering value propositions, as well as effective tactics like incentive programs and inventory management.

At this stage, we will do our own postmortem on the product development process. Where do organizations commonly run into trouble? They all have the same textbooks on marketing, and their factories may look similar. Yet success can be elusive. Why?

Wishful Thinking Is Not a Strategy

In high school, did you wish that you were more popular, hoping that the head cheerleader or football star would notice you? You probably learned that wishful thinking just doesn't cut it. Unfortunately, denial prevails as a management technique in many organizations.

In a famous *Harvard Business Review* article, C. K. Pralahad and Gary Hamel promoted the idea of viewing an organization through its core competencies, the production and logistical functions at which the company excels, and leveraging those into new markets,[3] much as an accountant presumably has the core competencies of math and analytical skills. We saw in Chapter 10 that Solectron's business may have been outsourced manufacturing electronics, but its expertise is really in global logistics management.

If you cannot see what your company truly does well, or if your company does not excel at any function that adds value, you are in deep trouble. Whether you are concerned with market positioning, staff capabilities, market share, or any other element of the business, you absolutely must assess it objectively and pay attention to that analysis. This is the step at which most companies fail—to the detriment of management and their shareholders.

Information Is Cheap but Expertise Is Not

Yes, anyone with an Internet connection can find a boilerplate contract, but how do you learn which clauses are most relevant to your industry or your situation? You can look up articles on market sizes, but what are the industry-specific pitfalls?

We are drowning in information today, but we're starving for interpretation. Data are easy to find and hard to decipher. Websites aggregate information but don't filter it. It has always been easy to find data to support a point ("This market is growing," or "Our competitor is dying"), but critical review is in short supply. As a result, an underground network of corporate Cassandras find themselves busier than ever as they counter floods of data with reasoned analysis.

There is only one solution to this dual problem of data overload and analysis famine: find expertise, pay a fair price, and use it liberally. This actually falls under a more general warning against being penny-wise and pound-foolish. Whether they are engaged as employees or consultants, always hire the best people you can find and inspire them to stay.

Risk Analysis Is Not Old-Fashioned

Every 10 years, we believe that risk is gone and risk analysis is obsolete. The 1990s brought the tech boom and bust; 10 years later, some believed that housing prices would go up forever. So-called sophisticated investors traded shares in complex arrangements that amplified risk instead of mitigating it. Risk became a contagious disease; like a diffusing technology, it began with a few innovative adopters and spread even to conservative, risk-averse populations.

Managers typically underestimate their own risks. Sales managers fret that there isn't enough inventory, while operations managers worry about the sales effort keeping up. CEOs agonize over investor meetings, believing internal affairs to be under control. Every ambitious business plan contains a disclaimer stating that "these are conservative projections." Don't be fooled! Your own area is subject to as much uncertainty as any other.

What About *Me*?

One of my first clients said something interesting to me: "In business school, you learn all about delivering value to shareholders and other nice ideas, but at the end of the day, management is most concerned with keeping their jobs." Cynical but true.

Should you be concerned? Probably. The developing world is filled with millions of people who are smart, hungry, and extremely ambitious. In almost every recruiting engagement I have had recently, the most significant limitation on hiring the sharpest candidates has been their immigration status. In comparison, American students are complacent and entitled—and they see themselves as first in line to be the next generation of managers. Even worse, the recession has inspired government to take up the employment slack, maintaining a mind-set that works against being competitive. But economic cycles will remain a reality, and the private sector rebound will reward relentless focus.

You need to be better prepared and smarter than ever. Soak up all the training you can and keep your hand on the pulse of your market. If your only concern is keeping your job, then you will not have it for long.

PRODUCT DESIGN PRINCIPLES

Design sensibilities change with time, just like hairstyles and politics. Our priorities change with the environment. Infant car seats motivated automakers to build cars with special tether systems. Rising gas prices helped lift sales of hybrid cars. Things change.

While products change dramatically (does anyone want to see my original *Thriller* album?), needs don't really change much. I still listen to music. People use e-mail or text messaging instead of the phone, but they still reach out to their friends and coworkers. What are some age-old principles—and even truisms—that can keep you competitive today?

Every Decision Is a Value Proposition

Every day we determine whether something is "worth it" as we analyze the world around us. We are constantly looking for return on every aspect of our lives: Should I call this customer or that one this morning? Who is more likely to place a purchase order sooner? Is it worth it to pull my kid out of day care half an hour early if I work after he goes to bed? What's the point of calling my brother if we'll have an unpleasant conversation? Is it worth it?

As Adrian Ott writes in her book *The 24-Hour Customer*, "Time isn't money. It's more important than money."[4] (Read Ott's book for a number of strategies to market effectively in this environment.) Chapter 8 showed you the resource triangle, demonstrating that we can only allocate money, time, and people. That's it; that's all we have to work with. We are constantly trading back and forth between these three resources, looking for returns. We hire salespeople, trading money for people, and then wait for them to sell products to generate a return. We hire assistants, trading money for people again; their return is measured in time when we can leave work early. We subconsciously evaluate the value of every cent and every minute that we spend.

Smart managers constantly evaluate people too; but it's easier to redeploy time and money to new activities than it is people. Just as you are looking for a return, so are your customers, your vendors, your employees, and everyone around you. (Some would say even your kids are in this mind-set.) How do you cope with this? There are two strategies.

First, provide value—as much as you can, all the time. Reach out to your customers. Offer advice and educate them. Reach into your network to meet their other needs. On the flip side, look for returns on everything you do. Exercise ruthless prioritization over all your resources. Scrutinize your calendar. Avoid pointless Internet-surfing. Spend marketing dollars wisely. Is it worth it? The answer to anything you do should be yes.

Plug-and-Play Is a State of Mind

After years of watching computers grow in complexity, we have actually entered an era of startling simplicity. Google's Web page has become an icon of stark functionality, dominated by the box where we, the users, literally input what we seek. The hit Flip video camera changed the world of home movies by making filming as easy as taking a picture.

"Plug-and-play" began as a phrase describing the addition of peripherals to a computer system, but it now describes our expectation for integrating any new technology or even a person into our lives. We hire consultants because we expect them to have little or no learning curve. Companies grow by acquisition in hopes of adding immediately to their top line and seeking synergies (that is, ways to share costs). We look for vendors based on turnkey solutions so that we can get on to the next task.

This is harder than it looks. In 2009, Cisco acquired Pure Digital, the maker of the Flip video camera, for $590 million. But the Flip's simple style stands alone in the vast Cisco universe, and the company has struggled to integrate this ethos into the rest of its consumer lineup.[5] Do you think of "simple to use" as a Cisco trademark? Neither do I.

Plug-and-play is a state of mind. Your product should work immediately when someone boots up, logs in, switches on, or signs up.

Learn from (Instead of Foisting onto) the Developing World

When your business model crashes, don't expect the developing world to save you. Many managers have shown their supervisors the proverbial hockey stick revenue projection, demonstrating how introducing a product in China will cause sales to skyrocket.

Consider Kodak's monumental arrogance in trying to save its film business this way when digital cameras took off. Kodak management had plenty of time to see the approaching train. As early as 1981, when Sony announced the first prototype digital camera, Kodak management realized that film photography would come to an end.[6] By 2004 (23 years later!), the transition had gained speed: 31 percent of American families had a digital camera, and the percentage was expected to increase to 42 percent within a year. As a result, Eastman-Kodak predicted a decline in U.S. consumer film sales of 10–12 percent[7]—and yet the company still hoped to generate growth of 8–9 percent in film sales to China and India.[8] Talk about hubris! Kodak has yet to recover from this colossal misstep,[9] and it is certainly unlikely to see the margins it had from its film business again.

On the other hand, you can use the developing world as an inspiration for new business models. As mentioned in Chapter 2, GE leveraged its innovation capabilities with an interesting case. When management discovered that the standard $100,000 ultrasound machine would not be practical in China because people could not travel to standard imaging centers where these machines are typically housed, the company instead developed a new portable unit for $15,000. The goal was to learn how to make products with "50 percent functionality at 15 percent of the price."[10]

The developing world is not going to settle for our hand-me-downs. These growing societies demand equality of opportunity and should be taken seriously as a market and a catalyst for new ways of doing business.

CUSTOMER RELATIONSHIPS

The information revolution has largely removed the information asymmetry that characterized business for most of history. Consumers can determine the average price points in the marketplace by looking at Craigslist or industry-specific sites like Carfax. Research in business-to-business sales consists of extracting volumes of information from annual reports and publicly available market research. Rumors circulate rapidly on the Internet. Everyone largely knows what everyone else is doing.

As a result, your customers are meeting you on a level playing field: ignore them at your peril. Specifically, how can you harness their energy? Which roles do they play in your organization?

Customers Are Designers Who Pay You

As you've seen throughout the book, Apple, Google, Cisco, Zara, and many other leading corporations illustrate that the path to success is to include customer participation early in the design process. Henry Ford would be laughed out of the room today for saying that a car can be "any color, as long as it's black." The same innovative adopters described in Chapter 11 as the targets of your new product launch demand that you accommodate their needs early in the process.

When I first moved to Pasadena, the streets were crawling with people recruiting audience members for movie screenings. Studios would release an early version, show it for free, and collect audience feedback. Today, we beta test all kinds of products. Like the movie studios, we want to pick the ending the audience will love.

In the most extreme case, you can customize your product. One example is Blank Label, a manufacturer that allows customers to design their own shirts, from collar to cuff, color to style. It is part of a growing trend in Internet ventures that minimize their inventory costs by customizing manufacturing.[11] (This also creatively manages working capital, since the customer pays before manufacturing commences, although presumably the company has the materials in stock.)

Tailor your product when you can. Look to your customers to help you. Take a lesson from the movie *Jerry Maguire*, where the sports agent says, "Help me help you." Everyone benefits.

Customers Have Large Networks but Tight Circles: Use Them Both

It is now easier than ever to get market research, yet companies still fail to reach their markets every day. Why?

We may have wide networks but tight circles. In fact, we only have a loose association with most of the people to whom we're linked. Even though we're bombarded with e-mails, commercials, telemarketers, and other unsolicited communication, we still have the same number of close friends as before.

Use that to your advantage to open doors and create real relationships with your potential clients and prospective customers. Three-martini lunches have changed, but the need for socialization hasn't. Learn what your customer needs for his bonus, what your consumer wants to simplify her life. There is no substitute.

Similarly, the information revolution has made it possible for your clientele to participate in the marketing process. The innovative adopters are also your grassroots sales force. If they don't like how you have broadcast your value, they will reshape your message and distribute it throughout your network. Innovative adopters have always served as advocates, but until recently they could not sell to the masses as effectively as a corporation because they lacked the funds to mount an advertising campaign. YouTube and Facebook have changed all that.

Whether you like it or not, your customers are part of your sales force. Unhappy readers will speak out against an author, and disappointed consumers can mount electronic riots on Web servers. Listen to your customers.

Customers Know as Much (or More) About the Market as You Do

If you have gotten a new medication recently, you may have searched for it on the Internet to learn about the side effects and maybe even different pricing at various pharmacies. Similarly, car buyers walk into a Honda dealership knowing how many 2007 Odysseys are on the lot and the average selling price for the last six months. This is true in every industry. Your customers probably know more than you do at every turn.

Historically, marketing has concerned itself more with creating customers than retaining them, but with access to so much information, customers need not be as loyal to a brand. It is insufficient to earn your customer's trust once; you must work to keep it.

What can you do? It's simple: be fair and never take your customers for granted. Incentivize people and businesses to try your service or product, and reward them for taking the risk. Assume that they will leave if there is a problem, so work to retain them.

HINTS FOR ENTREPRENEURS

Because I work closely with so many small companies, I have a special place in my heart—and thus in this book—for entrepreneurs. So I have a few final hints for you who are boldly going to start new companies. Are you scared? You should be; it is scary indeed! However, keep in mind that André Gide, the 1947 Nobel Laureate, said, "Man cannot discover new oceans unless he has the courage to lose sight of the shore."

Booms and Busts Are Both Good for Business

With the recession, entrepreneurs started to moan that it was a terrible time to start a business. You might be less depressed if you consider that companies started during recessions include Hewlett-Packard (1939), Starbucks (1971), Microsoft (1975), and Apple (1977).

It's fun to be an entrepreneur in a boom. You get favorable deal terms, a healthy valuation, and fast closes on your deals. Who can complain? On the other hand, when the tables turn, it becomes challenging to deliver the return to your investors. Meanwhile, investors love busts because they can get more for every dollar.

A realtor friend told me that he appreciates downturns because they flush out the competition. You can learn to appreciate the improved opportunities in a recession. It is easier to hire good people, you can get great deals on space to house your growing company, and your vendors are more flexible because they too need to close their deals. Exploit downturns.

Your Competition Is Every Other Deal on the Table

Chapters 3 and 4 touched on the fact that your product doesn't just compete against products in your space; in the funding world, you compete against other deals on the table. If you are involved in a capital allocation exercise, each division has pet projects competing for the CEO's attention. In an angel financing environment, software entrepreneurs could be competing against movie studios or shoe manufacturers; every active deal is a threat to you.

Raise money with a conscientious marketing campaign, using the entire alphabet soup presented in this book—the marketing Four Ps, the advertising Five Ms—and all the other tools at your disposal. Think of your return on investment as the value proposition for your investors. Create a deal with competitive advantage.

Be a Young Big Company, Not a Small Business

Don't think like a small company, be a young big one. Perhaps you have heard people say, "Dress for the job you want, not the one you have." Guess what? It doesn't apply just to clothes. Market in a fashion consistent with the company you will become, and don't be foolish. Use nice paper for traditional mailings and good grammar in your e-mails. Articulate your strategy, admitting what you don't know, and seek guidance from your investors.

Most important, the missing ingredient from most small businesses is accountability. No one is responsible for failure, but everyone gets credit for success. Unfortunately, all companies must go through growing pains—and the key one is developing a mature organization. Demand accountability of yourself and those around you. Don't create a country club for your friends.

KEYS TO THE KINGDOM

It is time to finish your product development. Many a parent has sent a young adult into the world, unsure if their child is ready but hoping for the best; your product may be in a similar situation. There may be features you meant to add, alternatives you had hoped to explore. Unfortunately, you cannot do everything at once.

Postmortems help you wrap up the project so you can repeat the right activities and avoid systemic problems the next time around. Focus these meetings on data instead of personal attacks. Use trained outside facilitators who won't play favorites and will create a safe environment in which everyone can speak freely.

Think about the exciting journey ahead of you and the one behind you. Seek clarity from data, not just from opinions. Manage your people, money, and time carefully. Even as the world is shrinking, your competition is growing; ambition is global, and like it or not, every product can create or destroy a relationship.

Act with integrity, find trustworthy employees who are in harmony with your values, take care of your customers, and your business will thrive. Good products stem from creative environments—and in the end, this requires the right people.

Chapter Quiz

1. Customers today are _____ .
   a. irrelevant
   b. part of your sales force
   c. a waste of time
   d. strategically unnecessary
2. Recommended behaviors for postmortems do *not* include being
   _____ .
   a. proud
   b. factual
   c. professional
   d. brief
3. *Core competencies* refer to the _____ .
   a. intellectual property portfolio
   b. production functions at which a company excels
   c. older products that were foundations for new ones
   d. corporate weaknesses
4. *Plug-and-play* refers to _____ .
   a. the need to use all your resources at once
   b. vertical integration
   c. rapid development of intellectual property
   d. a mind-set of delivering instant value

5. In downturns, the one thing you should *not* do is _____ .
   a. find good deals in renting space
   b. hire good people
   c. create good arrangements with vendors
   d. postpone your investors' needs

6. Strategies for the developing world should focus on _____ .
   a. delivering older product lines with low demand in developed nations
   b. educating consumers to adopt higher-cost solutions
   c. developing creative business models around new product economics
   d. outsourcing processes without generating sales

7. Entrepreneurs should *not* _____ .
   a. plan to be a large company
   b. consider marketing theory in pitching a deal
   c. think about competitive advantage in creating a deal
   d. minimize the time spent creating a company

8. Suggestions for successful postmortem exercises do *not* include which of the following?
   a. Blaming the people responsible for problems
   b. Creating positive and negative balance
   c. Using quantifiable data
   d. Varying the format

9. Tailoring your product is _____ .
   a. never recommended
   b. a growing trend
   c. not economical
   d. impossible

10. Management solutions to data overload and analysis famine include which of the following?
    a. Limit your time on the Internet.
    b. Spend all your time analyzing the data.
    c. Find and pay for expertise.
    d. Limit your dependence on data.

ANSWER KEY

Chapter 1

1. d
2. a
3. d
4. b
5. c
6. c
7. d
8. b
9. a
10. b

Chapter 2

1. a
2. d
3. d
4. c

5. c
6. a
7. b
8. c
9. b
10. a

Chapter 3

1. c
2. d
3. b
4. b
5. a
6. d
7. b
8. c
9. a
10. c

Chapter 4

1. b
2. c
3. b
4. b
5. c
6. d
7. a
8. d

9. c
10. a

Chapter 5

1. a
2. c
3. d
4. a
5. b
6. c
7. c
8. d
9. b
10. c

Chapter 6

1. b
2. a
3. d
4. c
5. a
6. d
7. b
8. c
9. c
10. d

Chapter 7

1. c
2. a
3. b
4. c
5. d
6. d
7. a
8. b
9. a
10. c

Chapter 8

1. a
2. d
3. c
4. c
5. b
6. d
7. a
8. b
9. a
10. d

Chapter 9

1. d
2. c

3. b
4. a
5. d
6. a
7. c
8. a
9. d
10. b

Chapter 10

1. b
2. c
3. b
4. c
5. d
6. a
7. b
8. d
9. a
10. b

Chapter 11

1. c
2. a
3. b
4. b
5. d
6. c
7. d

8. b
9. a
10. a

Chapter 12

1. b
2. a
3. b
4. d
5. d
6. c
7. d
8. a
9. b
10. d

NOTES

INTRODUCTION

1. "Industry Overview: Grocery Stores and Supermarkets," Hoovers, hoovers.com/grocery-stores-and-supermarkets/--ID_84--/free -ind-fr-profile-basic.xhtml, 2010, viewed May 20, 2010.

2. Norman Herr, "Television and Health," Internet Resources to Acompany *The Sourcebook for Teaching Science*, 2007, www .csun.edu/science/health/docs/tv&health.html, 2007.

CHAPTER 1

1. *Bloomberg BusinessWeek*, www.*BusinessWeek*.com/interactive _reports/innovative_50_2009.html.

2. *Bloomberg BusinessWeek*, www.*BusinessWeek*.com/magazine/ content/06_17/b3981403.htm.

3. Satish Nambisan and Mohanbir Sawhney, "A Buyer's Guide to the Innovation Bazaar," *Harvard Business Review*, June 2007, 109–118.

4. U.S. Small Business Administration Office of Advocacy, "Frequently Asked Questions," U.S. Small Business Administration, September 2009, http://sba.gov/advo/stats/sbfaq.pdf.

CHAPTER 2

1. Michael E. Porter, "The Five Competitive Forces That Shape Strategy," *Harvard Business Review*, reprint R0801E, January 2008, exed.hbs.edu/assets/shape-strategy.pdf.

2. W. Chan Kim and Renée Marbourgne, *Blue Ocean Strategy* (Boston: Harvard Business School Press, 2005).

3. Larry Huston and Nabil Sakkab, "Connect and Develop: Inside Procter & Gamble's New Model for Innovation," *Harvard Business Review*, March 2006, http://hbr.org/2006/03/connect-and -develop/ar/1.

4. Jeffrey R. Immelt, Vijay Govindarajan, and Chris Trimble, "How GE Is Disrupting Itself," *Harvard Business Review*, reprint R0910D, October 2009, lombardglobal.com/attachments/hbr_how_ge_is_ disrupting_itself.pdf.

5. http://money.cnn.com/magazine/fortune/bestcompanies/snap shots/957.html.

6. Robert Spector and Patrick McCarthy, *The Nordstrom Way to Customer Service Excellence* (New York City: John Wiley, 2005).

7. Tess Gadwa, "Building a Sales Culture," *Charlotte Business Journal*, March 5, 2004, www.bizjournals.com/charlotte/ stories/2004/03/08/focus1.html.

8. Kim and Marbourgne *Blue Ocean Strategy*.

CHAPTER 3

1. Philip Kotler and Kevin Lane Keller, *Marketing Management*, 12th ed. (Upper Saddle River, NJ: Pearson Education, Inc., 1994), 37.

2. David Phillips, "General Motors Has Ruled the Road, but Not Without Enduring Its Share of Dents," *Detroit News*, August 13, 2008, http://detnews.com/article/20080813/AUTO01/808130486/

General-Motors-has-ruled-the-road--but-not-without-enduring
-its-share-of-dents#ixzz0vlj6NPjW.

3. Kotler and Keller, *Marketing Management*, 19–20.

4. Richard Wise and Peter Baumgartner, "Go Downstream: The New
    Profit Imperative in Manufacturing," *Harvard Business Review*,
    September-October 1999, http://hbr.org/1999/09/go-downstream/
    ar/1.

CHAPTER 4

1. Adrian C. Ott, *The 24-Hour Customer* (New York City: Harper-
    Collins, 2010).

2. Damon Darlin, "Applause Please, for Early Adopters," *New York
    Times*, May 9, 2010.

3. Saul Hansell, "Is There a Method in Cellphone Madness?" *New
    York Times*, November 14, 2009.

CHAPTER 5

1. Kevin G. Rivette and David Kline, *Rembrandts in the Attic: Un-
    locking the Hidden Value of Patents* (Boston, MA: Harvard Busi-
    ness School Press, 2000), 108–109.

2. Catherine J. Holland, Vito A. Canuso III, Diane M. Reed, et al.,
    Intellectual Property (Canada: Entrepreneur Media, 2007).

3. Rivette and Kline, *Rembrandts in the Attic*, 111–113.

4. Sheldon Mak and Rose Anderson, "Selecting and Protecting
    Trademarks" (pamphlet), 2008.

5. "2008 Patent Litigation Study: Damages Awards, Success Rates
    and Time-to-Trial," PricewaterhouseCoopers, 2009.

6. Sheldon Mak and Rose Anderson, "Managing Intellectual Prop-
    erty: 10 Recommendations for Protecting What Belongs to You"
    (pamphlet), 2008.

7. Marie C. Baca, "Counterfeit-Goods Sting Nabs Tourist-Spot Ven-
    dors," *Wall Street Journal*, August 4, 2010, pA6.

8. Ross Epstein, "Licensing and Distribution Agreements: Who
    Should Chase the Counterfeiters?" *LES Insights*, 2010.

CHAPTER 7

1. Bala Iyer and Thomas H. Davenport, "Reverse Engineering Google's Innovation Machine," *Harvard Business Review*, reprint R0804C, April 2008, http://usefullunacy.typepad.com/useful_lunacy/files/HBR_Google_Mar2008.pdf.

2. Scott Austin, "Cisco Acquired Most Start-Ups In Decade, But Oracle King In '09," January 5, 2010, *Wall Street Journal* Blogs, http://blogs.wsj.com/venturecapital/2010/01/05/cisco-acquired-most-start-ups-in-decade-but-oracle-king-in-09/tab/article.

3. Maria Shao, "Cisco Systems, Inc.: Collaborating on New Product Introduction" (Stanford Graduate School of Business Case GS-66, Board of Trustees of the Leland Stanford Junior University, 2009).

4. Everett M. Rogers, *Diffusion of Innovation*, 4th ed. (New York: The Free Press, 1995), 143.

5. Richard M. Gomez, "Centralized Command–Decentralized Execution: Implications of Operating in a Network Centric Warfare Environment" (thesis, Air War College, Air University, 2003).

6. Steven E. Prokesch, "How GE Teaches Teams to Lead Change," *Harvard Business Review*, January 2009, http://hbr.org/2009/01/how-ge-teaches-teams-to-lead-change/ar/1.

7. Malcolm Gladwell, *The Tipping Point* (Boston, MA: Little Brown, 2000).

8. Alan Deutschman, "The Fabric of Creativity," *Fast Company*, December 1, 2004, fastcompany.com/magazine/89/open_gore.html.

9. Stefan Thomke and Ashok Nimgade, "IDEO Product Development" (Harvard Business School Case Study 9-600-143, President and Fellows of Harvard College, April 26, 2007).

10. Robert Spector and Patrick McCarthy, *The Nordstrom Way to Customer Service Excellence* (Hoboken, NJ: John Wiley & Sons, 2005), 6.

11. Eric von Hippel, Stefan Thomke, and Mary Sonnack, "Creating Breakthroughs at 3M," *Harvard Business Review*, reprint 99510, September-October 1999, netscope.com/pdf/HBR.pdf.

12. Vijay Govindarajan, "Nucor Corporation" (Tuck School of Business at Dartmouth Case Study 2-0015, Trustees of Dartmouth College, 2000).

13. Nanette Byrnes, "Pain, But No Layoffs at Nucor," *BusinessWeek*, March 26, 2009, *BusinessWeek*.com/magazine/content/09_14/b4125054802295.htm.

14. Jim Collins, *Good to Great: Why Some Companies Make the Leap . . . And Others Don't* (New York: HarperCollins, 2001).

CHAPTER 8

1. J. Carey, "What's a Fair Price for Drugs," *BusinessWeek*, April 30, 2001, 105–106.

2. "Vioxx Recall May Cost Merck $2 Billion," *Forbes*, October 1, 2004, *Forbes*.com/2004/10/01/1001automarketscan01.html.

3. Stefan Thomke and Ashok Nimgade, "IDEO Product Development" (Harvard Business School Case Study 9-600-143, President and Fellows of Harvard College, April 26, 2007).

4. *Defense Acquisition Guidebook*, U.S. Department of Defense, https://dag.dau.mil/Pages/Default.aspx.

5. Maria Shao, "Cisco Systems, Inc.: Collaborating on New Product Introduction" (Stanford Graduate School of Business Case GS-66, Board of Trustees of the Leland Stanford Junior University, 2009).

CHAPTER 9

1. "Flextronics: A Focus on Design Leads to India" (Stanford Graduate School of Business Case OIT-45, 2005, Board of Trustees of the Leland Stanford Junior University, January 10, 2005).

2. Stefan Thomke and Ashok Nimgade, "IDEO Product Development" (Harvard Business School Case Study 9-600-143, President and Fellows of Harvard College, April 26, 2007).

3. Ali Farhoomand, "Samsung Electronics: Innovation and Design Strategy" (Asia Case Study, University of Hong Kong, Ref. 09/410C, Poon Kam Kai Series, 2009).

4. Stefan Thomke and Barbara Feinberg, "Design Thinking and Innovation at Apple" (Harvard Business School Case Study 9-609-066, President and Fellows of Harvard College, rev. May 19, 2009).

5. P. E. Teague, "Special Achievement Award: Jeff Hawkins," *Design News*, March 6, 2000, 108.

6. Eric von Hippel, Stefan Thomke, and Mary Sonnack, "Creating Breakthroughs at 3M," *Harvard Business Review*, reprint 99510, September-October 1999, netscope.com/pdf/HBR.pdf.

7. Bruce Nussbaum, "The Power of Design," *BusinessWeek*, May 17, 2004, *BusinessWeek*.com/magazine/content/04_20/b3883001_mz 001.htm.

8. Deishin Lee and Lionel Bony, "Cradle-to-Cradle Design at Herman Miller: Moving Toward Environmental Sustainability" (Harvard Business School Case Study 9-607-003, President and Fellows of Harvard College, rev. December 16, 2009).

9. Forest Reinhardt, Ramon Casedus-Masanell, Debbie Freier, "Patagonia" (Harvard Business School Case Study 9-703-035, President and Fellows of Harvard College, rev. January 20, 2010).

10. Patagonia, "Company Information: Mission Statement," http://patagonia.com.

CHAPTER 10

1. Kasra Ferdows, Michael A. Lewis, and Jose A. D. Machuca, "Rapid-Fire Fulfillment," *Harvard Business Review*, November 2004, http://hbr.org/2004/11/rapid-fire-fulfillment/ar/1.

2. John Powell, "Understanding the Trends That Have Shaped Detroit," The Kirwan Institute for the Study of Race and Ethnicity, Ohio State University, October 4, 2005.

3. Maria Shao, "Cisco Systems, Inc.: Collaborating on New Product Introduction" (Stanford Graduate School of Business Case GS-66, Board of Trustees of the Leland Stanford Junior University, June 5, 2009).

4. Cisco, "Corporate Overview," November 2009, cisco.com.

5. "Solectron: From Contract Manufacturer to Global Supply Chain Integrator" (Stanford Graduate School of Business Case GS-24,

Board of Trustees of the Leland Stanford Junior University, November 2, 2001).

6. Margo E. K. Reder, "How Apple's Business Model Controls Digital Content Through Legal and Technological Means," *Journal of Legal Studies Education* 26, (2009): 185–209, http://ssrn.com/abstract=1085702.

7. Apple, "iTunes Store Top Music Retailer in the US," press release, April 3, 2008, apple.com.

8. "Intuit Inc.: From Products to Services in the Information Age" (Stanford Graduate School of Business Case GS-21, Board of Trustees of the Leland Stanford Junior University, rev. May 17, 2007).

9. Ferdows, et al., "Rapid-Fire Fulfillment."

CHAPTER 11

1. Everett M. Rogers, *Diffusion of Innovation*, 4th ed. (New York: The Free Press, 1995), 11.

2. Geoffrey A. Moore, *Crossing the Chasm* (New York City: HarperBusiness, 1999).

3. Susan Fournier and Robert J. Dolan, "Launching the BMW Z3 Roadster" (Harvard Business School Case Study 9-597-002, President and Fellows of Harvard College, January 8, 2002).

4. "Developing and Marketing a Blockbuster Drug: Lessons from Eli Lilly's Experience with Prozac" (Stanford Graduate School of Business Case BME-6, Board of Trustees of the Leland Stanford Junior University, February 25, 2005).

5. Craig Smith, Robert J. Thomas, and John A. Quelch, "A Strategic Approach to Managing Product Recalls," *Harvard Business Review*, September-October 1996, http://hbr.org/1996/09/a-strategic-approach-to-managing-product-recalls/ar/1.

6. Susan Tifft and Lee Griggs, "Poison Madness in the Midwest," *Time*, October 11, 1982, http:www.time.com/time/magazine/article/0,9171,922991-2,00.html.

7. Judith Rehak, "Tylenol Made a Hero of Johnson & Johnson: The Recall That Started Them All," *New York Times*, March 23, 2002.

8. N. R. Kleinfeld, "Tylenol's Rapid Comeback," *New York Times*, September 17, 1983.

9. Laurie Flynn, "Intel Facing a General Fear of Its Pentium Chip," *New York Times*, December 19, 1994.

10. "Intel Adopts Upon-Request Replacement Policy on Pentium Processors with Floating Point Flaw; Will Take Q4 Charge Against Earnings," *Business Wire*, December 20, 1994, http://findarticles .com/p/articles/mi_m0EIN/is_1994_Dec_20/ai_15939945.

CHAPTER 12

1. Ed Catmull, "How Pixar Fosters Collective Creativity," reprint R0809D, *Harvard Business Review*, September 2008, http:// corporatelearning.hbsp.org/corporate/assets/content/Pixararticle .pdf.

2. "Learning from Projects: Note on Conducting a Postmortem Analysis" (Harvard Business School Case Study 9-600-021, President and Fellows of Harvard College, September 3, 1999).

3. C. K. Pralahad and Gary Hamel, "The Core Competence of the Corporation," *Harvard Business Review*, product 6528, May–June 1990, http://tle-inc.com/PDFS/FILES/resources/The%20 Core%20Competencies%20of%20the%20Corp.pdf.

4. Adrian Ott, *The 24-Hour Customer: New Ways for Winning in a Time-Starved, Always Connected Economy* (New York: Harper-Collins, in press).

5. Andy Greenberg, "Cisco's Gadget Guru," *Forbes*, May 10, 2010, http://www.*Forbes*.com/*Forbes*/2010/0510/technology-flip-cam corder-puredigital-cisco.html.

6. Giovanni Gavetti, Rebecca Henderson, and Simona Giorgi, "Kodak and the Digital Revolution (A)" (Harvard Business School Case Study 9-705-448, President and Fellows of Harvard College, rev. November 2, 2005).

7. Mike Cline, "One Hour Film Processing," SBDCNet San Antonio, July 26, 2004, http://sbdcnet.org/dmdocuments/2004PhotoLab. pdf.

8. "Kodak Unveils New Strategy," *The Economist*, January 22, 2004, http://globaltechforum.eiu.com/index.asp?layout=printer_friendly&doc_id=6948.

9. "A Tense Kodak Moment," *BusinessWeek*, October 17, 2005, *Business Week*.com/magazine/content/05_42/b3955106.htm.

10. Jeffrey R. Immelt, Vijay Govindarajan, and Chris Trimble, "How GE Is Disrupting Itself," *Harvard Business Review*, reprint R0910D, October 2009, lombardglobal.com/attachments/hbr_how_ge_is_disrupting_itself.pdf.

11. Amy Wallace, "Putting Customers in Charge of Design," *New York Times*, May 16, 2010.

INDEX

INSTRUCTIONS FOR ACCESSING ONLINE FINAL EXAM

I f you have completed your study of *The McGraw-Hill 36-Hour Course: Product Development*, you should be prepared to take the online final examination. It is a comprehensive test, consisting of 100 multiple-choice questions. You may treat this test as an "open book" exam by consulting this book and any other resources. Answers to the online exam can be found on The McGraw-Hill 36-Hour Course Information Center landing site for each book (please see the instructions below for accessing the site).

Instructions for Accessing Online Final Exam
1. Go to www.36hourbooks.com.
2. Once you arrive on the home page, scroll down until you find The McGraw-Hill 36-Hour Course: Product Development and click the link "Test your skills here." At this point you will be redirected to The McGraw-Hill 36-Hour Course Information Center landing site for the book.

3. Click the "Click Here to Begin" button in the center of the landing site. You will be brought to a page containing detailed instructions for taking the final exam and obtaining your Certificate of Achievement.

4. Click on "Self-Assessment Quiz" in the left-hand navigation bar to begin the exam.

ABOUT THE AUTHOR

Andrea Belz, an expert in technology commercialization, has provided strategic and operational guidance in innovation to global leaders, including General Electric, Best Buy, NASA's Jet Propulsion Laboratory, and the California Institute of Technology. Her blog discussing the venture capital industry and global innovation has been cited by the *Wall Street Journal, USA Today*, and others; she has been interviewed by CNN.com, Fund Strategy, Global Corporate Venturing, and many leading news organizations.

Andrea has spoken at the California Institute of Technology, the University of Southern California, Pepperdine University Graziadio School of Business, HRL Laboratories, International Law Seminars, the Product Development Management Association, and many other organizations. She chairs a session on technology commercialization for the industry-leading IEEE Aerospace Conference and is a member of the Licensing Executives Society. A long-time member of the Pasadena Angels, Andrea has worked closely with many venture capital funds and private equity groups in managing their portfolio companies.

Andrea holds a B.S. in physics from the University of Maryland at College Park, where she was named the Outstanding Undergraduate in Computer, Mathematical, and Physical Sciences; an M.B.A. in finance from the Pepperdine University Graziadio School of Business; and a Ph.D. in physics from the California Institute of Technology. She lives in Altadena, California, with her family.